chinese
astrology

JONATHAN DEE

Previously published in 2006 as *Simply Chinese Astrology* by
Zambezi Publishing Limited, Devon, UK

This edition first published in Great Britain in 2017 by
Orion
and imprint of the Orion Publishing Group Ltd
Carmelite House, 50 Victoria Embankment,
London, EC4Y 0DZ
An Hachette UK Company

1 3 5 7 9 10 8 6 4 2

Interior design by Kathryn Sky-Peck

A CIP catalogue record for this book is available
from the British Library.

Paperback ISBN: 978 1 4091 6959 8

eBook ISBN: 978 1 4091 6960 4

Printed and bound by CPI Group (UK), Ltd, Croydon, CR0 4YY

Contents

An Introduction to the 12 Animals

Chinese Astrology is a tradition that stretches back in time over several thousand years. It developed into an extremely complex set of systems, some of which are so difficult that our moderns minds can no longer cope with the complexity. Even the Chinese themselves had problems dealing with it in the past, so they developed a simplified version around the 2nd century AD. This is the system of the twelve animal signs with which we in the Western hemisphere have become familiar.

The word "zodiac" is derived from the Greek *zōidiakos*, literally meaning "circle of figures." In the Western world, our version of the zodiac includes several human figures such as Gemini, Virgo, and Aquarius as well as animals. In Chinese terms, each of the 12 signs is represented by an animal. The signs begin with the Rat who is followed by the Ox, the Tiger, the Hare, the Dragon, the Snake, the Horse, the Goat, the Monkey, the Rooster, the Dog, and finally the Pig.

There is a charming legend to account for why these particular animals were chosen in this precise order. It seems that long ago, the ruler of the universe (some say Buddha or Lao Tzu, others say the August Personage of Jade) decided that all the animals that were of service to man should run a race to establish the signs of the zodiac. The Rat received his invitation to attend and told the other animals; however the Cat was worried that he might over-sleep, so he made the Rat promise to wake him in plenty of time. This was a task that the Rat neglected to do, so the Cat never made it to the starting line, and is the reason why cats loathe rodents to this day. On the morning of the race, the Rat and ten other animals lined up ready to begin, knowing that the first one to reach the feet of the Supreme Being would have the honor of becoming the first sign. The Supreme Being noticed that one animal was absent, so he sent his advisor down to earth to find an extra contestant. The very first animal the advisor encountered was a small, fat pig. Without further ado, he seized the animal and brought it to the starting line.

Finally, all was ready, set, and go. At first the swifter beasts such as the Dragon, Horse, and Tiger kept a fast lead, but they soon became tired and fell behind. The tenacity of the Ox proved to be a winning trait as he shouldered the Tiger aside; it looked as though the Ox was going to be the victor. But just as the Ox was about to reach the winning line, the cunning Rat—who had concealed himself in Ox's tail—ran over the Ox's back and jumped off the end of his nose. The Supreme  Being was very impressed by the Rat's ingenuity but was still not sure that he had won the race fairly. To clinch the matter, the Rat produced a flute and began to play and dance, which amused the Almighty and persuaded him to award the honor to the shrewd Rat. By the time the Rat had finished his antics, the fat little Pig finally waddled up in last position. And that is how the order of the zodiac signs was established.

Your
Chinese
Horoscope

1

A question that many people ask is "how can Chinese astrology be relevant if one sign lasts a whole year?" The answer, of course, is that there is more to it than that. Like any other form of astrology, Chinese astrology operates on different levels, and the most basic of these is the study of the animal that rules your year of birth. A slightly more complex feature involves the Yang/Yin polarity of the year and the element that rules it. Apart from that, there is the question of which animal governs one's birth moon and the animal that influences one's hour of birth. Professional astrologers in China take into account a great deal more than this, including the day of birth and the lunar cycle that one was born in, but in this book we'll keep things simple.

The good news is that Chinese astrology does not require any complicated calculations. It can provide a shortcut to a greater understanding of yourself, your inner nature, and your destiny.

The Chinese Year

The first thing you will need to do is to look up your sign according to your year of birth. The Chinese use a lunar calendar, so the start of the Chinese year changes from one year to the next. If you were born in January or February, you must pay special attention to the calendar, because you were born around the time when one sign ends and the next begins. If you were born right on the cusp of two signs, read both descriptions, and see which fits you best.

Many Chinese people are so tuned in to the Chinese calendar, that if you say, "I was born under the sign of the Tiger," they would immediately know the year of your birth. They would not remember the actual start date for that year, so they would fall back on a generalized date of February 4, which is sometimes called the "Imperial New Year." Some Chinese astrologers actually prefer using February 4, and that is fine in most instances, but when someone is born around the time of the New Year, they like to know exactly which sign is really theirs, and with the aid of this book, you can do the job properly.

The chart on pages 4–7 gives the start dates of the Chinese years, each year's polarity (Yang or Yin, active or passive), its ruling element and its animal sign.

Look at your year of birth in the table and note down your polarity, element, and animal. For example, someone born in 1977 would be a Yin Fire Snake.

The Animal Moon

The next thing to do is to work out your animal moon, which links to your month of birth. This is even easier because it links with our familiar Western zodiac. Consult the chart on page 8 to find your animal moon.

For example, if you happen to be a Virgo then you were born in the Moon of the Rooster, and if you are a Sagittarius then you were born in the Moon of the Rat.

Putting the Chinese year and animal moon together: someone who was born on June 2, 1982 was born in the year of the Yang-Water-Dog in the Moon of the Horse. A person born on November 25th in 2001 is born in the year of the Yin-Metal-Snake in the Moon of the Rat.

Year	Start Date	Type	Element	Animal Sign
1930	January 29	Yang	Metal	Horse
1931	February 17	Yin	Metal	Goat
1932	February 6	Yang	Water	Monkey
1933	January 25	Yin	Water	Rooster
1934	February 14	Yang	Wood	Dog
1935	February 3	Yin	Wood	Pig
1936	January 24	Yang	Fire	Rat
1937	February 11	Yin	Fire	Ox
1938	January 31	Yang	Earth	Tiger
1939	February 19	Yin	Earth	Hare
1940	February 8	Yang	Metal	Dragon
1941	January 27	Yin	Metal	Snake
1942	February 15	Yang	Water	Horse
1943	February 4	Yin	Water	Goat
1944	January 25	Yang	Wood	Monkey
1945	February 12	Yin	Wood	Rooster
1946	February 2	Yang	Fire	Dog
1947	January 22	Yin	Fire	Pig
1948	February 10	Yang	Earth	Rat
1949	January 29	Yin	Earth	Ox
1950	February 16	Yang	Metal	Tiger
1951	February 6	Yin	Metal	Hare
1952	January 26	Yang	Water	Dragon

CHINESE ASTROLOGY PLAIN AND SIMPLE

Year	Start Date	Type	Element	Animal Sign
1953	February 14	Yin	Water	Snake
1954	February 3	Yang	Wood	Horse
1955	January 24	Yin	Wood	Goat
1956	February 11	Yang	Fire	Monkey
1957	January 30	Yin	Fire	Rooster
1958	February 18	Yang	Earth	Dog
1959	February 7	Yin	Earth	Pig
1960	January 28	Yang	Metal	Rat
1961	February 15	Yin	Metal	Ox
1962	February 5	Yang	Water	Tiger
1963	January 25	Yin	Water	Hare
1964	February 13	Yang	Wood	Dragon
1965	February 1	Yin	Wood	Snake
1966	January 21	Yang	Fire	Horse
1967	February 9	Yin	Fire	Goat
1968	January 29	Yang	Earth	Monkey
1969	February 16	Yin	Earth	Rooster
1970	February 6	Yang	Metal	Dog
1971	January 26	Yin	Metal	Pig
1972	February 15	Yang	Water	Rat
1973	February 3	Yin	Water	Ox
1974	January 24	Yang	Wood	Tiger
1975	February 11	Yin	Wood	Hare

Year	Start Date	Type	Element	Animal Sign
1976	January 31	Yang	Fire	Dragon
1977	February 18	Yin	Fire	Snake
1978	February 7	Yang	Earth	Horse
1979	January 28	Yin	Earth	Goat
1980	February 16	Yang	Metal	Monkey
1981	February 5	Yin	Metal	Rooster
1982	January 25	Yang	Water	Dog
1983	February 13	Yin	Water	Pig
1984	February 2	Yang	Wood	Rat
1985	February 20	Yin	Wood	Ox
1986	February 9	Yang	Fire	Tiger
1987	January 29	Yin	Fire	Hare
1988	February 17	Yang	Earth	Dragon
1989	February 6	Yin	Earth	Snake
1990	January 26	Yang	Metal	Horse
1991	February 14	Yin	Metal	Goat
1992	February 3	Yang	Water	Monkey
1993	January 22	Yin	Water	Rooster
1994	February 10	Yang	Wood	Dog
1995	January 31	Yin	Wood	Pig
1996	February 19	Yang	Fire	Rat
1997	February 7	Yin	Fire	Ox
1998	January 28	Yang	Earth	Tiger

Year	Start Date	Type	Element	Animal Sign
1999	January 16	Yin	Earth	Hare
2000	February 5	Yang	Metal	Dragon
2001	January 24	Yin	Metal	Snake
2002	February 12	Yang	Water	Horse
2003	February 1	Yin	Water	Goat
2004	January 22	Yang	Wood	Monkey
2005	February 9	Yin	Wood	Rooster
2006	January 29	Yang	Fire	Dog
2007	February 18	Yin	Fire	Pig
2008	February 7	Yang	Earth	Rat
2009	January 26	Yin	Earth	Ox
2010	February 14	Yang	Metal	Tiger
2011	February 3	Yin	Metal	Hare
2012	January 23	Yang	Water	Dragon
2013	February 10	Yin	Water	Snake
2014	January 30	Yang	Wood	Horse
2015	January 20	Yin	Wood	Goat
2016	February 8	Yang	Fire	Monkey
2017	January 28	Yin	Fire	Rooster
2018	February 15	Yang	Earth	Dog
2019	February 4	Yin	Earth	Pig
2020	January 24	Yang	Metal	Rat

Zodiac Sign	Dates	Chinese Moon
♈ Aries	March 21—April 20	Moon of the Dragon
♉ Taurus	April 21—May 21	Moon of the Snake
♊ Gemini	May 22—June 22	Moon of the Horse
♋ Cancer	June 23—July 23	Moon of the Goat
♌ Leo	July 24—August 23	Moon of the Monkey
♍ Virgo	August 24—September 23	Moon of the Rooster
♎ Libra	September 24—October 23	Moon of the Dog
♏ Scorpio	October 24—November 22	Moon of the Pig
♐ Sagittarius	November 23—December 21	Moon of the Rat
♑ Capricorn	December 22—January 20	Moon of the Ox
♒ Aquarius	January 21—February 19	Moon of the Tiger
♓ Pisces	20 February—20 March	Moon of the Hare

The Animal Hours

Just as the animal signs relate to particular years and months, they also correlate to the hours of the day. More precisely, each of the twelve animal signs equates to a two-hour period during the course of twenty-four hours, as shown in the chart on page

Simply use the time at your place of your birth. There is one small proviso: a birth during Daylight Savings Time or British Summer Time needs to have one hour subtracted. Thus 1:30 am becomes 12:30 am—or the hour of the Rat.

	Animal Sign	Hours
	Rat	11 pm—1 am
	Ox	1 am—3 am
	Tiger	3 am—5 am
	Hare	5 am—7 am
	Dragon	7 am—9 am
	Snake	9 am—11 am
	Horse	11 am—1 pm
	Goat	1 pm—3 pm
	Monkey	3 pm—5 pm
	Rooster	5 pm—7 pm
	Dog	7 pm—9 pm
	Pig	9 pm—11 pm

Yang and Yin

2

By now you should know what yearly animal sign you were born under, as well as the element for that year, and whether that element is Yang or Yin. Your Western birth sign should tell you what animal moon you were born under and thus reveal your emotional nature. The hour of your birth (if known) will then show your general temperament and possibly the "face" that you show to the outside world.

To understand what all these pieces of information mean, we will have to start with the basics beginning with the fundamental concepts of Yang and Yin.

Positive or Negative

Chinese philosophy is based on the idea of balance between two forces. These are known as Yang and Yin. Yang is thought of as masculine, positive, light and energetic. Its opposite, Yin is considered feminine, negative, dark and passive.

A common error that many people make is to think of Yang as "good" and Yin as "bad." Nothing could be further from the truth. It is better to think of Yang and Yin as an interplay of forces, each of which is nothing without reference to its opposite. These opposites express themselves as day and night, summer and winter, hot and cold, light and dark and so on, including every pair of conceivable opposites that exist. People too, are basically Yang or Yin by nature. This, according to Chinese astrology is dictated by polarity of the year in which one was born. If there were no Yang type people in the world there would be no progress, enthusiasm, sport, exploration, activity or indeed any change at all. Without Yin people there would be no routine, no tasks completed, farms and business would be neglected, children would not be cared for and tradition and continuation would cease.

Each of the animal signs is considered to be either Yang or Yin in nature. As one might expect, people born under Yang signs are assertive, active, extrovert and courageous. They may also be inclined to impulse, foolhardiness and be apt to "throw their weight around." People who are born under Yin signs are more receptive, patient, subtle and adaptable. They have the ability to endure but they may also be prone to negative thoughts and fall prey to depression when times are tough.

Animal	Polarity
Rat	Yang
Ox	Yin
Tiger	Yang
Hare	Yin
Dragon	Yang
Snake	Yin
Horse	Yang
Goat	Yin
Monkey	Yang
Rooster	Yin
Dog	Yang
Pig	Yin

The
Elements

3

The elements are at the heart of Chinese astrology and unfortunately are the most confusing aspect of it. There are five elements: Wood, Fire, Earth, Metal, and Water, and they are always listed in that order.

While each of the twelve animals rules one year, the elements preside over *two* consecutive years. For example, 1994 was the year of the Yang-*Wood*-Dog and 1995 was the year of the Yin-*Wood*-Pig. The elements are considered neutral and thus able to change their Yang/Yin polarity.

The animal signs repeat every twelve years but they are modified by the change of element in each sequence. To illustrate this point, let us look at the Rooster:

1957	The year of the Fire Rooster
1969	The year of the Earth Rooster
1981	The year of the Metal Rooster
1993	The year of the Water Rooster
2005	The year of the Wood Rooster

The entire sequence of animal signs and element combinations is only complete when sixty years have passed so it will not be the Year of the Fire Rooster again until 2017. During each sixty-year cycle, each animal will have been linked with all five of the elements.

In the Western world we tend to put the main emphasis on the animals of the Chinese zodiac; however, for the Chinese, the five elements are equally important. Traditional Chinese thought holds that the element governing a particular year provides a sort of shorthand to the nature of that year. So a year governed by Metal will be thought to be difficult with more than its fair share of challenges, while a year of the Water element will be good for commerce, the economy, and business in general. So ignoring the animal signs for a moment, someone can be described as a Wood, Fire, Earth, Metal, or Water person.

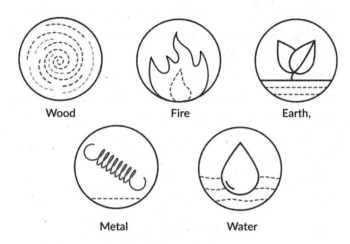

Wood   Fire   Earth,

Metal   Water

Elements and the Planets

Chinese astrology is not primarily concerned with the heavenly bodies in the same way that western astrology is, so the following information is just for interest's sake:

Jupiter is called the Wood Planet

Mars is called the Fire Planet

Saturn is called the Earth Planet

Venus is called the Metal Planet

Mercury is called the Water Planet

The sun and the moon are called the "Great Yang" and the Great Yin" respectively. The outer planets Uranus, Neptune and Pluto are invisible to the naked eye so they do not appear in the traditional Chinese system.

Incidentally, the more complex forms of Chinese astrology do involve the study of the planets, stars, the Milky Way, the moon and its phases and eclipses and much else that is familiar to western astrologers and astronomers. However, the information became increasingly confined to a small band of specialists within the Emperor's court and it was kept away from the masses lest they become too knowledgeable. As each regime came and went, some encouraged the use of astrology in court circles and some outlawed it. The result is that true astrology and astronomy became absorbed into the strangely idiosyncratic form that we know today.

The Creation Cycle

The elements are more correctly called "Agents of Change." They each express a state of being at a particular moment in an ever-changing universe. The ancient Chinese gave them their names because each one reminded them of a particular stage of "change" or, as we would call it "evolution."

- We begin with Wood, which provides fuel for the next element, Fire.
- In turn the remnants of Fire, namely ash, goes back to the Earth.
- In the depths of the Earth, Metal is born.

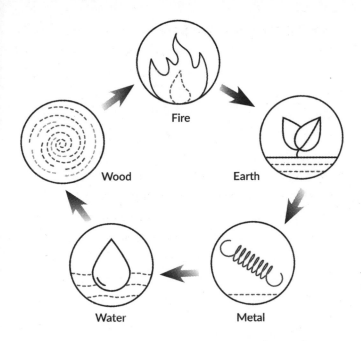

Fire

Wood   Earth

Water   Metal

- Metal when molten flows like Water. Equally when Metal is in solid form condensation is likely to form on it and Water is encountered again.
- Water of course is taken in through the roots of plants to form Wood.

However this is not the only way in which the elements can interact. Another sequence has more sinister overtones. Wood can drain Earth, Earth can befoul Water, Water can douse Fire, Fire can melt Metal and Metal can chop Wood. This is known as the "Destruction Cycle."

The Destruction Cycle

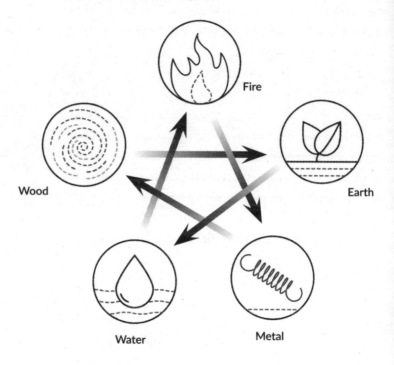

Fire

Earth

Metal

Water

Wood

- Wood exhausts Earth
- Earth pollutes Water
- Water douses Fire
- Fire melts Metal
- Metal chops Wood

These relationships between the elements have a relevance to a person's fortunes. For instance if one were born in a year governed by the Wood element, then a Metal year would not be very lucky because Metal chops Wood. Equally a Water person would not be too happy in a year governed by Earth, because Earth muddies Water. On the other hand, years that belong to one's own element are said to be lucky.

Of course in the traditions of Chinese astrology some signs are considered to be compatible while other signs are considered enemies. So the prospect of adding an elemental bias also adds another complication. For instance those born under the Rooster are considered to be compatible with those born under the signs of the Ox and the Snake. However if the Rooster in question happens to be of the *Fire* element he will find that an Ox or Snake who is of the *Wood* element will tend to encourage him, and this elemental mix will enhance the relationship. This is because Wood fuels Fire in the Creation Cycle. On the other hand, our Fire Rooster is likely to experience a few problems with an Ox who is of the Water element because this Ox will tend to dampen the Rooster's enthusiasm. The reason for this is because the combination of Fire and Water form part of the Destruction Cycle.

The same principle applies to individual years, so an Earth ruled person will not have such good fortune in a Wood year (Wood exhausts Earth). This is an important point to remember because even if the animal year is compatible to your own sign; its element may not be, and this will moderate the fortunes that you can expect during that year.

On a more positive note, the opposite is also the case. If you find yourself in an animal year that is incompatible with your own sign, then your bad luck may be lessened by that year's favorable element.

- Wood element people will be happy during Wood years because they will be good for them, as indeed will years governed by Water or Fire. However Earth and Metal years are likely to be difficult.
- Fire element people will find fortune in Fire years and also in Wood and Earth years while years governed by Metal and Water will present problems.
- Earth element people will find that Earth, Fire and Metal years are more fortunate than Water and Wood years.
- Metal element people will find that Metal, Earth and Water years suit them while Wood and Fire years do not.
- Water element people will be luckier in Water, Metal and Wood years but not quite so happy in years governed by Fire and Earth.

The Natural Elements of the Animals

The ancient Chinese considered each of the animal characters of their zodiac to have a natural inclination toward either Yang or Yin, and to also have a natural preference for a particular element. This is despite the fact that each of the signs will, during a sixty-year cycle, experience both polarities and be influenced by each of the five Elements.

This study of the natural elements of the animals takes us beyond the "plain and simple" scope of this book, but for those who wish to pursue further study, an overview of the correspondences is added here. The following is a list of the "preferences" of each animal.

- Rat naturally prefers Yang and the Water element

- Ox naturally prefers Yin and the Earth element

- Tiger naturally prefers Yang and the Wood element

- Hare naturally prefers Yin and the Wood element

- Dragon naturally prefers Yang and the Earth element

- Snake naturally prefers Yin and the Fire element

- Horse naturally prefers Yang and the Fire element

- Goat naturally prefers Yin and the Earth element

- Monkey naturally prefers Yang and the Metal element

- Rooster naturally prefers Yin and the Metal element

- Dog naturally prefers Yang and the Earth element

- Pig naturally prefers Yin and the Water element

Meanings of the Elements

At the start of each element, you will find the "correspondences."
Once you know your element, you can include the colors, shapes,
compass directions and other factors into your home or place of
business to make it suit your Chinese element nature and bring
you luck. You can even plant the right kind of tree in your garden
if you are fanatical enough about such things!

Wood People

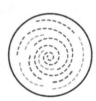

When Yang	Oak
When Yin	Willow
Field when Yang	Intellect
Field when Yin	Knowledge
Seeks	Wisdom
Comportment	Achiever
Body Shape (Yang)	Raw-boned
Body-Shape (Yin)	Slender
Aided by	Water
Hindered by	Metal
Lucky Day	Thursday
Lucky Season	Spring
Lucky Planet	Jupiter (Wood Planet)
Lucky Color	Green
Lucky Direction	East
Lucky Shape	Rectangle

Those born in periods influenced by the Wood element tend to be intellectual—philosophers, teachers, students, lawyers, and doctors. Education is very important to Wood people; these people are usually inclined to careers in computing, electronics, science, and communications. Many Wood people are deeply interested in philosophy, and are inclined to religion and spirituality. Wood tends to give a clear value system and high standards. This element also implies an influential position and ethical practices. The Wood element will add compassion and caring to whatever characteristics the year's animal sign might bring.

First Wood Year—Yang: Known as "Oak"

People born in a Yang Wood year are very clever and astute. Indeed there is very little point in attempting to fool them because the motives of others are generally clear to them. An Oak type person is hard working, responsible, self-motivated and possesses sound judgment. They will thrive anywhere that an organized mind and quick thinking are required. However, they do need to be left to their own devices and to do things their own unique way without interference. In personal terms, it is important to be honest with an Oak because they will not forgive deceit or emotional blackmail.

Second Wood Year—Yin- Known as "Willow"

As the name implies the Willow type of person tends to bend in the wind. These people are extremely impressionable and possess great empathy. It is very likely that a Willow person will consistently put other people's needs before their own. This trait can cause them to lose out in the long run simply because they didn't pay enough attention to their own interests. Willow people are often shy or modest, rarely asking for recognition. In romance they can be too trusting and often find themselves in a position of vulnerability. In China it is believed that Willows are very highly placed in terms of spiritual merit.

Fire People

When Yang	Blaze
When Yin	Flame
Field when Yang	Activity
Field when Yin	Enterprise
Seeks	Fame
Comportment	Showman
Body Shape (Yang)	Powerful
Body-Shape (Yin)	Wiry
Aided by	Wood
Hindered by	Water
Lucky Day	Tuesday
Lucky Season	Summer
Lucky Planet	Mars (Fire Planet)
Lucky Color	Red
Lucky Direction	South
Lucky Shape	Triangle

The element of Fire was associated with the warriors of ancient China. Fiery types are courageous, and are likely to be found in the public eye in movies, television or on the stage, or in the military, fire or police services. Fire people are often crusaders, having made a particular cause their own. Often they will publicly identify themselves with their personal cause because this element has an association with uniforms, badges and insignia. Being born in a Fire year adds strength, assertion energy and passion to the character. However, recklessness and impatience are also likely.

First Fire Year—Yang: Known as "Blaze"

Blaze type people are warriors who charge at everything. This is not someone who messes about—they get right to the core of the matter at hand. Blaze types are open and can be uncomfortably forthright. They are impatient, often with a short fuse and a hot temper. They are extremely brave, so if action is needed, the Blaze person is the one to call. They are very clever and quick to pick up new ideas, but impatience can be their downfall; they don't often consider the feelings of those around them and thus can easily make enemies. Traditionally, people born in Blaze years make excellent cooks.

Second Fire Year—Yin: Known as "Flame"

People born in Yin Fire years provide a steady flame, unlike the fierce conflagration of the Blaze type. Flame people are showmen by nature, and are likely to be found in the media or on the stage. Usually less demanding and adventurous, Flame people prefer a glamorous lifestyle. The Flame person is always the center of attention, dazzling the audience with personality and witty repartee. However, there is a sub-group of the Flame type: the smooth-talking con artist who is out to take advantage of the gullible. In general, Flame people have an instinctive understanding of the public mood and will adapt themselves to appeal to it.

Earth People

When Yang	Grassland
When Yin	Farm
Field when Yang	Industry
Field when Yin	Service
Seeks	Security
Comportment	Still
Body Shape (Yang)	Stocky
Body-Shape (Yin)	Stocky
Aided by	Fire
Hindered by	Wood
Lucky Day	Saturday
Lucky Season	The equinoxes
Lucky Planet	Saturn (Earth Planet)
Lucky Color	Yellow
Lucky Direction	Center, Southeast, Northeast
Lucky Shape	Square

In keeping with the earthy nature of this element, people born in Earth years are traditionally held to be excellent builders, farmers and keepers of water buffaloes. Even in modern times the associations haven't changed much, the areas of expertise being construction, manufacturing, farming and food production generally. The Earth element is a stabilizing influence, adding practicality, business acumen, a generous nature and often a very long memory. Earth people are patient, prudent and conventional. The character of an Earth born person is placid, slow to anger but unforgiving of a hurt. However, it does increase the ambition of these efficient souls and grant considerable administrative abilities.

First Earth Year—Yang: Known as "Grassland"

Grassland people, born in the Yang Earth year are generally conventional and in tune with their particular society. Usually physically strong, possessing a capacity for hard work and often possessed of a talent for leadership. It is this latter trait that can lead to a position of authority and honor. Grassland types have an honest and earthy manner. They are sensual and "earthy" in sexual affairs. However, they do tend to lack a romantic sense and prefer reliability and stability in relationships to empty but pleasing gestures of affection. The best opportunities are found in banking, insurance, finance and security industries.

Second Earth Year—Yin: Known as "Farm"

All Earth born people are hard workers and the Yin type is no exception. Farm types may project a negative aura of suspicion but they too will tend to find success in life. Traditionally, this type is supposed to lack imagination, so that they often ignore opportunities if the benefits are not immediately obvious. Farm people are not quite as ambitious as the Grassland type. In general, Farm people prefer to find a comfortable niche in life and then happily stay there for many years. In other words, Farm people like being in a rut. On the other hand, many Farm people are artistically gifted and express their talents by creating beautiful things.

Metal People

When Yang	Steel
When Yin	Ornament
Field when Yang	Management
Field when Yin	The Arts
Seeks	Status
Comportment	Graceful
Body Shape (Yang)	Balanced
Body-Shape (Yin)	Curvaceous
Aided by	Earth
Hindered by	Fire
Lucky Day	Friday
Lucky Season	Autumn
Lucky Planet	Venus (Metal Planet)
Lucky Color	White
Lucky Direction	West & Northwest
Lucky Shape	Oval, circle

Metal people tend to be more independent than other elemental types and unwilling to rely on others; the are "a law unto themselves." While this can be an advantage, it can also make Metal types aloof, proud, and self contained; it's important for them to emerge from self-imposed isolation once in a while. Those born in a Metal year are determined, stubborn, unyielding, and somewhat hard on themselves and on others. Once a course of action is decided upon Metal people will stick to it come what may, even when it is obviously a hopeless cause.

First Metal Year—Yang: Known as "Steel"

At first impression the Steel person appears to be aloof and a natural aristocrat. Those born in a Yang Metal year will easily win respect and admiration but may also tend to put on a few airs and graces because they consider themselves to be a cut above the common throng. As might be imagined, status is very important to this type. Many Steel people have something of a head start in life with families who provided them with all the tools necessary for later success. Even if this is not the case, people of Steel will progress up the ladder of success very quickly indeed. In affairs of the heart, Steel types are as determined in this arena as they are in all others, but once their goal is attained they may swiftly cool, become bored and callously move on.

Second Metal Year—Yin: Known as "Ornament"

The Ornament or Yin Metal person is as much a natural aristocrat as his Steel counterpart, but the charm and the "noblesse oblige" that nobility implies is more obvious. This is an idealistic person to whom fair play is very important. Indeed, an Ornament person will fight for the right and often involves himself in social movements and good causes. In affairs of the heart, Ornament types can be rather shy, often rather brittle and will tend to shy away from commitment. The Yin Metal person is thoughtful and will be seen to be doing the right thing, whatever that may be. He is capable of making affectionate gestures but under the shiny metallic exterior he really yearns for independence.

Water People

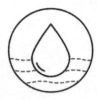

When Yang	River
When Yin	Fishing Net
Field when Yang	Liquid Assets
Field when Yin	Fixed Assets
Seeks	Wealth
Comportment	Flexible
Body Shape (Yang)	Rounded
Body-Shape (Yin)	Rounded
Aided by	Metal
Hindered by	Earth
Lucky Day	Wednesday
Lucky Season	Winter
Lucky Planet	Mercury (Water Planet)
Lucky Color	Black
Lucky Direction	North
Lucky Shape	Wavy Lines

In Western astrology, the Water element is connected to the emotions, but this is not so in the East. In China the element of Water is strongly connected to communication, and to matters of finance and commerce. Traditionally those born in a Water year tend to be tax collectors, merchants, landlords, bankers, and accountants. However, Water people are not always successful with money; if they do lose a large sum, they can usually make it all back again and learn from their mistakes. Water types are intuitive and communicative, and can be quite soft and tolerant. They possess a natural ease of expression and are often envied by more socially awkward people. Emotionally, Water people are very sensitive and can be easily hurt. If they are unhappy in love, they tend to compensate by becoming workaholics.

First Water Year—Yang: Known as "River"

Those born under the influence of Yang Water are clever, talented, hard workers with an eye for opportunity. However, this can sometimes be a problem because they never know when to stop working. They possess excellent public relations skills and are natural diplomats, capable of diffusing difficult situations. River people can spot a gap in the market and then work very hard to fill it. They are also capable of rescuing an ailing business and turn it into a thriving concern. However, romantically River people can be very fickle. Some can be quite promiscuous. Many of their relationships will feature a notable age gap between partners.

Second Water Year—Yin: Known as "Fishing Net"

Fishing Net people are gentle, intuitive and emotionally vulnerable. However, being Water, there is still that ever-present knack for business and finance. The Fishing Net type tends to lack an independent streak, so a career in a larger organization would be preferable to charting an individualistic course. This type needs encouragement to thrive. Fishing Net people tend to conceal their true feelings and this often makes them seem enigmatic. These are extremely romantic people, sincere and loyal in their affections and very sexy indeed. Many of this type have had a rough time in their relationships and need to develop a more positive self-image.

The Rat

4

(1936, 1948, 1960, 1972,

1984, 1996, 2008, 2020)

In contrast to the western world's opinion of rodents, the Rat is considered to be the sign of charm. This is not the vile rat of the sewers but a raider of bulging granaries. The sign symbolized by this opportunistic scavenger is a fortunate one noted for shrewdness, enterprise and the accumulation of wealth.

The Virtues of the Rat

Charming, protective, dynamic, communicative, compassionate, skilful, upright, attractive, idealistic, prosperous, experimental, talented, adaptable, open-minded, entrepreneurs

The Vices of the Rat

Talkative, obsessive, defensive, addictive, fickle, exploitative, anxious, mean, opinionated, bossy

The Rat Personality

Those born in the year of the formidable Rat are shrewd, intelligent, impatient, assertive and very conscious of their own self-interests. However, hard-working Rat personalities are rarely unpleasant, in fact they are noted for immense charm, social grace and an excellent sense of humor. Tasteful, refined and stylish, the popular Rat is a person to be noticed. On the more negative side,

Rats love to gossip, are very critical both of themselves and others, and they can be prone to petty attitudes and greed.

It is said that the Rat's fortunes will be better if he was born at night or during the summer months. A Rat born in the daytime will be less enterprising and more fearful.

The Rat in Love

Rat personalities are extremely devoted to those who they love, sometimes obsessively so. This can be taken to extremes with the Rat carrying a flame for someone who does not reciprocate his fond feelings. He is generous and selfless to those he adores and he does not hesitate to reveal the depths of his feelings. Emotionally the Rat experiences many highs and lows in his relationships. He is therefore rather fragile and vulnerable. This is because he can be too open about himself and while young, he may reveal too many personal details to abusive types of people. It will take some time but eventually the Rat person will find the love of his life, one who will give him the emotional support and affectionate security that he craves.

The Rat's Lovers, Friends, and Enemies

The Rat is likely to find romance with those born under the signs of the Ox, the Monkey, and the Dragon.

He will find companionship with the personalities of Tigers, Snakes, and Pigs, and comfort with other Rat personalities, even though there will be some friendly rivalry within the relationship. Although the Rat and the Dog will get on as friends, a marriage between these two would not be wise.

Goat and Horse personalities loathe the Rat on sight. Roosters will be irritating to the Rat but with a little give and take they may tolerate each other eventually.

The Rat Career

Many Rats are extremely ambitious and career minded. Energetic, shrewd and versatile, Rats can weave their way past all obstacles and achieve stunning success. Rat personalities are extremely complex, so beneath their veneer of confidence hides a nature that is prone to anxiety; one that cannot accept failure and that fears the mockery of the world at large. This gives a Rat person an enormous drive to succeed. Your money had better be on the Rat even when he is faced with seemingly appalling odds.

Many Rats find fulfillment as writers and many have a great interest in history.

The Rat and the Five Elements

People born in Rat years are also influenced by one of the elements of Chinese tradition. This adds a further influence to their already complex personalities.

The Wood Rat (1984)

This Rat is very shrewd and forward-looking. His insight is such that he is aware of upcoming trends and will usually be way ahead of his time. This is an excellent and eloquent communicator. The Wood Rat is charming, romantically inclined and usually artistically gifted. He may have known poverty in youth and endured a difficult early life. He is therefore in need of security and emotional support.

The Fire Rat (1936, 1996)

The fiery type of Rat has a fast, witty and often caustic tongue. He is a crusader by nature and is never happier than when fighting tooth and nail for a worthy cause. He is motivated by very strong ideals and possesses and honorable character. He longs for excitement and revels in life's dramas. However, when life is dull this Rat is usually bored and despondent.

The Earth Rat (1948, 2008)

Money, and lots of it, really matters to the earthy type of Rat. This is probably a compensating factor for poverty in early life. This Rat will work very hard to gain security, and he has enough strength of purpose to achieve his ambition. His need for security often leads to a disastrous early marriage. Later partnerships tend to be better, after the Earth Rat has achieved some prosperity. Only then can they establish a happy family unit.

The Metal Rat (1960, 2020)

This is an idealistic, perfectionist Rat. Like his fellow rodents, the metallic Rat is shrewd in business but may be too conscious of money matters to the detriment of his relationships. His emotional life is likely to be turbulent and he may be prone to jealousy. Metal Rats often posses an athletic physique and their innate charm is best expressed to a wide audience.

The Water Rat (1972)

This is an intellectual, deep thinking Rat who inspires respect. The Water Rat is a diplomat who can cleverly get his own way without offending anyone else. He is a little too critical and his cool exterior can make him appear unfeeling, which is not the case. He is an intrepid traveler but he will be happiest when he journeys with a good companion who loves and understands his complex nature.

The Year of the Rat

This is the first year of the animal zodiac cycle and it should begin with growing enthusiasm and a sense of optimism. The Rat favors the opportunist, so those with the perception to spot a gap in the market should do very well under the influence of this shrewd rodent. In other words, if there is something that you have always yearned to do, but if you have never found the opportunity to follow your dream, then find time during a Rat year! Having said that, it is not wise to race ahead regardless of consequences. Those who wish to progress will have to prepare for their new enterprise so that it will last beyond the end of the Rat Year.

The Rat is an irreverent creature, so those in authority will find themselves challenged over the course of this year. On the other hand, the creative arts should flourish.

The Fortunes of the Rat Year by Year

The Rat in the Rat Year: When found in its own year the Rat enjoys success and happiness almost beyond measure, no

obstacle will be to great for this amorous little rodent. The downside to this is that all this positive drive and energy may cause the
Rat to push his luck a little too far and receive short hard lesson
in humility in return!

The Rat in the Ox Year: Hard work is promised for a Rat during this year, but on the other hand, this enterprising little rodent
finds that this is second nature. Even when the struggle becomes
a daily grind the Rat instinctively knows that if he uses his head
his projects will have a successful outcome even if the challenges
are tough!

The Rat in the Tiger Year: When the Rat and Tiger meet head on
danger and uncertainties are the result. Situations that were once
safe will suddenly become insecure. Being a natural survivor, the
Rat could still find a path to safety avoiding the claws of the Tiger,
but only if the Rat learns to use all his skills correctly and to the
best possible advantage!

The Rat in the Hare Year: In oriental tradition the Hare is sometimes referred to as the Cat, and Rat will have to pit its wits
against another feline foe, but this time they will be more evenly
matched. It will be a difficult learning curve for the little rodent as
it finds itself, losing ground to a more cunning and unscrupulous
opponent!

The Rat in the Dragon Year: After a couple of difficult encounters, the Rat will find a new sense of balance and harmony in the
year of the Dragon. As long as the Rat doesn't try to run before
he can walk he will do well. Fate dictates a year of excitement as

new relationships develop leading to lasting friendships and possibly romance!

The Rat in the Snake Year: The respite offered by the Dragon quickly fades when Rat finds itself in the company of the predatory snake. Work and home life will seem increasingly stressful to the Rat, who is forced to find a little peace and quiet anywhere he can. It is advisable for the Rat to remain discreet and truthful in all situations and not be too trusting. In the Snake year, it is vital for the Rat to keep his wits about him.

The Rat in the Horse Year: If Rat has been prudent then the year of the Horse will be a happy one. If on the other hand Rat has squandered previous opportunities to put something away for a rainy day, then the year of the Horse will be more difficult. Either way this is likely to be an expensive time for Rat. Opportunities disappear and commitments mount. The Rat will have to rely on his natural cunning and swiftness to make the most out of the Horse year!

The Rat in the Goat Year: The creative Rat will positively blossom in the year of the Goat! Even the less creative rodents will fare well in this gentle, loving time. Painful memories and past failures will be soon forgotten as the Rat moves forward with a new sense of determination and confidence!

The Rat in the Monkey Year: Rats will enjoy a year in the company of the lively Monkey. Success is not hard to find and in most cases will just seem to happen spontaneously. Many exciting new situations and opportunities will present themselves in this stimulating year. Rats can finally put the past behind them and enjoy a stress free time with lots of pleasant surprises!

The Rat in the Rooster Year: When Rat meets Rooster the practicalities of life will seem troublesome as the Rat begins to wonder why he even bothers to keep up the struggle against the world. However, this depressive mood could soon be lifted if Rat keeps both eyes open as true and lasting love may well be waiting for him!

The Rat in the Dog Year: The everyday struggle, and oppressive practical commitments of the previous year are now over as troubles and difficulties fade away as Rat finally begins to shine, but close relationships won't fair so well and Rat will have to develop a romantic sensibility, to devote time and effort to keep the spark of love alive.

The Rat in the Pig Year: This will a very good year for the Rat, bank balances will grow, boosting confidence and leading to a hectic and fun-filled social life. There is every likelihood that this wealth will last, for in the Pig Year, the Rat's destiny is favorable to long-term investments and saving schemes that will pay dividends for a long time to come!

The Ox

5

(1937, 1949, 1961, 1973,
1985, 1997, 2009)

The Ox is the sign of Tenacity and represents enduring prosperity through continuing effort and determination. It is the symbol of the springtime, agriculture, fertility, power and muscular strength.

The Virtues of the Ox

Patient, contemplative, skilful, dextrous, confident, eloquent, authoritative, industrious, a careful planner

The Vices of the Ox

Chauvinistic, proud, petty, critical, eccentric, overly conservative, grumpy

The Characteristics of the Ox Personality

Ox people are traditionally thought to be physically robust and clever with their hands. They are open minded, practical people who take life in their stride and are seldom disturbed by the unexpected. The Ox person likes an orderly existence, free of stress and too much passion. Oxen are home loving and usually devoted to their families. They are also materialistic: loving comfort, good food, music, art and comfortable furniture, though this intrinsic materialism and love of comfort is rarely vulgar. Most Oxen have excellent taste and they will arrange their surroundings superbly. However, some Oxen allow the materialistic side of their nature to overwhelm their entire lives so they can become covetous and miserly.

The Ox in Love

Although Ox people are often very clever indeed, they do tend to be a little naïve in matters of love. Their cool nature makes it difficult for them to be ardent and demonstrative. However, once they have found a congenial mate who has unearthed and encouraged their innate sensuality they are completely loyal, faithful lovers who will rarely stray. In Oxen relationships, it is continuity rather than passion that counts.

The Ox will find happiness with those born in the years of the Snake, the Rooster and the Rat. Additionally, other Oxen will often prove compatible mates.

Dragons, Hares, Monkeys, and Pigs as well as other Ox personalities will be good company and supportive friends.

The Ox will feel threatened by the ferocity of the Tiger. Value-conscious Oxen will hate the extravagance of the Goat, be depressed by the pessimistic Dog, and made to feel inadequate in the presence of the extrovert Horse personality.

The Ox Career

The Ox is a diligent and meticulous worker with an eye for detail and a perfectionist tendency. He is happiest in a conventional profession, one with a recognized, traditional structure and a clear-cut system of promotion. Preferably this is a career that has titles such as "Head of Department," "Manager," and "Executive Director." Oxen are particularly suited to estate management, gardening, farming, medicine or religion. Oxen could also be cut out for a career in teaching, catering or the police force.

The Ox and the Five Elements

People born in Ox years are also influenced by one of the elements of Chinese tradition. This adds a further influence to their already complex personalities.

The Wood Ox (1985)

This is an Ox who is ethical above all else. He will be renowned for his honest dealings and integrity. The Wood element predisposes him to possess social graces and to be thoughtful, considerate and kind. He is a deep thinker but he is not afraid of new ideas. In fact many of his ideals are progressive. In material terms he is capable of attaining great wealth.

The Fire Ox (1937, 1997)

The Fire element adds charisma to the Ox personality. This is an Ox who is drawn to the heights. He is ambitious and possibly ruthless in attaining his aims. He is proud and will be determined to get his own way. He will find it easy to dismiss opposition as the envy of inferiors. To be fair to the Fire Ox, he is a hard worker and scrupulously honest and direct.

The Earth Ox (1949, 2009)

This is a very practical Ox. He is sincere, hard working, and very loyal. The Earth Ox person has a strong sense of purpose and will persevere through all sorts of difficulties with a dogged determination without complaint to finally arrive at his desired goal. He may lack imagination and might be considered unemotional but he possesses a good heart nonetheless. His main fault is obstinacy.

The Metal Ox (1961)

This is an extremely proud, often arrogant, type of Ox. He is extremely strong-willed and possesses a tough, determined character. He is not afraid of challenges and will give as good as he gets in confrontations. The early life is likely to have been difficult and early challenges will have given the Metal Ox a tough hide.

The Water Ox (1973)

The best description of a Water Ox person is one who enjoys material comfort but suffers from emotional impoverishment. This is a realistic Ox who makes the best out of even in the worst circumstances. He is patient, calm and reasonable. He is industrious and works well with others. Unfortunately, the Water Ox may be jealous and suspicious when in love.

The Year of the Ox

The sequence of the Animal signs enters a stable phase in the Year of the Ox. However, this is not an easy ride for the Ox teaches us the value of hard work, and the important lesson that we get the rewards of life in direct proportion to the efforts we have put into it. So, the lazy, feckless and those who have wasted previous opportunities will not be too happy as the world suddenly becomes a more demanding place. This is a good year to make advantageous contractual agreements. This also implies that it is an excellent year in which to get married. The general rule governing the Ox Year is this: if your plans have been well thought out and arrangements made previously (in the Year of the

Rat) then all will be well. Spur-of-the-moment decisions are not so favorable. Slow and steady progress is the hallmark of the Ox Year so patience is required. The results will be worth waiting for.

The Fortunes of the Ox Year by Year

The Ox in the Rat Year: A sense of companionship prevails in the Rat Year as the Ox finds himself in the presence of people with whom he has much in common. However these new bonds are unlikely to develop into romances. Intellectual relationships are favored and the Ox will find much to occupy his mind. Reunions with old friends are likely. There is plenty of work to be done in this period but this will be undertaken with a cheerful heart.

The Ox in the Ox Year: The Ox is well placed in its own year and will enjoy a carefree time of happiness and joy. The usual pressures of mundane life will seem insignificant in this onslaught of positive energy. The usually steady and dependable Ox may now be tempted to take a few risks, but this uncharacteristic behavior will soon pass allowing the Ox to make some far reaching decisions that will continue to pay dividends well into the future.

The Ox in the Tiger Year: This is not the best of years for Oxen. Complications will arise in all areas of life and major changes may occur as a result. Confusion and indecision may be rife, and all Ox can do in the face of adversity is to knuckle down and work on the things that are really important in his life!

The Ox in the Hare Year: The Ox and the Hare quickly grow bored in each other's company. The Ox should try to avoid any close relationships during this year, especially those with work colleges, as this may lead to irritation and feelings of inadequacy because others may seem to be stealing the glory. A change of image might help, a change of attitude certainly will!

The Ox in the Dragon Year: Another uncomfortable time is forecast when the Ox spends a year in the company of Dragon. Tension and stress take their toll as the persistent Ox finds himself in a struggle against ostentatious Dragon and it's unlikely that the Ox will win, at least in the early stage of the conflict. However, dogged determination will eventually pay off because even the Dragon will tire eventually. It would be best for the Ox to consider long-term goals rather than immediate ones, because the more distant goals are more likely to be achievable!

The Ox in the Snake Year: The Ox finds comfort in the company of Snake. Happiness and contentment will return as life takes on a steadier, more manageable pace. Finances will improve and a clever Ox will find time to put something away, and even make a considerable profit. The only fly in the ointment is that the evidence of the good life might be found in an expansion of the waistline!

The Ox in the Horse Year: The hard work and persistence will really pay off in a big way for Ox in the year of the Horse. Rewards for past efforts will be gratefully received as fate smiles sweetly on the Ox. He must ensure that complacency doesn't set in and be prepared to make a sudden decision if he is to take advantage of maximum opportunity. Remember, that if the Ox is too slow off the mark then he could be left behind.

The Ox in the Goat Year: Both being grazing animals, you might be fooled into think that this will be a happy time for Ox, but not so! Life will take on a dreamy feel. Things will seem indistinct and somehow unreal, leaving Ox with an uncharacteristic sense of vagueness. He must resist all urges to delay or to fantasise in this year or the poor Ox will experience one problem after another.

The Ox in the Monkey Year: Fortune should be generally quite good for the Ox during the Year of the Monkey, but the straight-forward thinking bovine will occasionally struggle to adapt quickly enough to rapid changes. A positive mental attitude will be very important in times of stress. Luckier Oxen may be blessed with an exciting new love affair.

The Ox in the Rooster Year: The Ox will feel immediately at home in the company of Rooster, as stability, order and progress are the watchwords during the year of this strutting fowl. The Ox's staid image may be finally dumped as the outgoing nature of the Rooster rubs off on the rather old fashioned and conserva-tive Ox, but be warned not to take this too far as personal and intimate relationships may suffer!

The Ox in the Dog Year: The personality of the Ox might feel the urge to migrate to pastures new. The desire to expand horizons will be now be irresistible and it is a wise Ox who will follow his instinct. This outgoing, adventurous urge provides a necessary next step on life's pathway for wherever it leads will be better than the circumstances that have been left behind!

The Ox in the Pig Year: Things speed up for the Ox as it chases after the Pig. But the Ox has found an ally in the sentimental Pig and relationships, whether personal or professional will prosper as the pace of life picks up. Expect a few raised eyebrows, as friends might be shocked to see how the image of the Ox is transformed in the Pig Year. Oxen should now indulge his own desires without worrying too much about other people's opinions.

The Tiger

(1938, 1950, 1962, 1974, 1986, 1998, 2010)

6

The Tiger is the sign of courage. Chinese tradition states that this ferocious beast received one stripe on his back for every animal that he defeated. The Tiger is symbolic of the West, the evening and the harvest. The mighty Tiger represents optimism, humanitarianism and valor.

The Virtues of the Tiger

Lovable, alluring, warm-hearted, honorable, independent, idealistic, humanitarian

The Vices of the Tiger

Rash, hot headed, reckless, quarrelsome, caustic, moody, rebellious, disobedient, irreverent

The Tiger Personality

Those born in the Year of the Tiger are fascinating personalities. The Tiger person is vain, sociable, kind, humorous and cheerful but never make the mistake of thinking that he is gullible or a fool. The Tiger's flippant façade conceals a wild and ferocious nature. He has inner strength and enormous ambition. He will never be content putting up with second best. The Tiger always has his eye on the top! He loves wealth and status but there he is also rebellious and he won't be able to abide the authority of anyone else for very long. The Tiger works hard and lives hard. His energies are awesome. He has expensive tastes so it's a good thing that he also has the capacity to make a lot of money. Unfortunately this headlong rush has its price. Tigers are prone to stress related ailments if they don't take the demands of their bodies seriously enough.

The Tiger in Love

The Tiger personality is pleasure seeking with enthusiasm for life and a love of variety. Therefore, with so much on offer, it is not surprising that the Tiger can be a fickle lover. He falls in love a thousand times and on each occasion he says, "This is the one!" It is; until boredom and predictability set in and the relationship becomes routine. Then it is time for the Tiger to roam again. However, people of independent character will attract the Tiger, especially those who "play hard-to-get." In essence the Tiger needs a partner who quietly admires him, one who is steady, consistent, practical and very understanding.

The Tiger may form fulfilling relationships with those born in the years of the Dragon, Horse, and Dog.

The adventurous Tiger will win popularity with Rats, Hares, Roosters, Pigs, and occasionally other Tigers.

The cautious Ox, guileful Snake, and chattering Monkey are threatened by Tiger's bluster and will tend to avoid him.

The Tiger Career

The Tiger is optimistic, determined and filled with initiative so he constantly seeks novelty and challenge in his work. A Tiger person is most often self-employed or runs his own business. However, any career that involves a variety of activities will win favor from the Tiger, especially if he is to be found in a leadership capacity. He has a talent for inspiring loyalty and the best effort from his subordinates so the typical place to find the Tiger personality is when he's in charge.

Tigers are particularly suited to careers in the travel industry, design, advertising or politics. Tigers are often drawn to a military life. They may become explorers, travel writers, journalists or captains of industry.

The Tiger and the Five Elements

The Five Elements of Chinese tradition also have an influence on the character of the ferocious Tiger

The Wood Tiger (1974)

Wood Tiger personalities love prominence and celebrity, often finding themselves in a position of great responsibility, whether they wanted to be or not! This type of Tiger is often so independent minded that he prefers to live alone. Usually creatively gifted, artistic, original and inventive, Wood Tigers will gain a respectable income and a considerable reputation. Family life may be a problem and an emotional distance with the parents may emerge.

The Fire Tiger (1986)

The Fire Tiger is an extremely devious person. He is very, very clever, perhaps a little too clever because his intricate plots and manipulations of others can backfire quite spectacularly. He possesses a vast range of general knowledge and, like most Tigers;

the fiery type enjoys the limelight and the company of celebrities. Fiery Tigresses are sexually passionate and fiercely loyal. They are however, possessive and prone to jealousy.

The Earth Tiger (1938, 1998)

This is a resourceful and hard working Tiger. He has had to be! In most cases Earth Tigers have had a difficult early life. This type usually leaves home young and claws his way up the ladder of success on his own. This is a person with excellent leadership qualities. He possesses sound judgement and is capable of inspiring loyalty. In relationship terms, the Earth Tiger is faithful and possessive.

The Metal Tiger (1950, 2010)

The Metal Tiger dominates those around him, but he may lack empathy and has a reputation for being constantly dissatisfied. There is no doubt that he is very lucky, especially with money but he is rarely content with his good fortune. This is an egoistic Tiger, witty, eloquent and passionate. He is likely to be a risk-taker and a gambler. Some Metal Tigers make millions, but they must take great care not to squander their fortunes.

The Water Tiger (1962)

The Water Tiger will gain a reputation for honest dealings in business and fickleness in love. This is a born businessman, resourceful, ambitious and persuasive. However the Water Tiger has difficulty in ending situations and moving on, so old problems often return to his life at inconvenient moments. This Tiger is in particular danger when he begins a relationship without ending his pervious liaison.

The Year of the Tiger

The twelve months governed by the ferocious Tiger could easily be described as the "year of Living Dangerously." The arrival of this fearsome jungle cat heralds a turbulent time so it's not easy for timid souls to live through it without experiencing a lot of anxiety. For those who desire a quiet life, it's best to sit tight and hope for the best as the storm rages. Those who will do best in this frantic year are people who abandon logic and cool, calm planning and rely on intuition. Those who act in an impulsive manner and are willing to take a risk will also tend to do well, simply because they are in sympathy with the adventurous Tiger nature. For this year it's best to keep an open mind, take each day as it comes, and catlike, be ready to pounce in any direction at a moment's notice.

The Fortunes of the Tiger Year by Year

The Tiger in the Rat Year: Money and resources will be something of a problem for Tigers in the Rat Year. It's time for the Tiger to tighten his proverbial belt. The Rat is far too practical to be swayed by an Tigerish revolutionary zeal so it is important to retain a sense of proportion, be sensible and if possible try and put something away for a rainy day!

The Tiger in the Ox Year: Another difficult year is forecast when Tiger and Ox meet. Arguments and conflicts will be rife simply because the Tiger is prone to over-confidence and likely to charge into a fight without considering the possibility that he might lose. Losing is a very likely outcome! The Tiger must think twice because sometimes it is better to bite his tongue and bide his time.

The Tiger in the Tiger Year: It is said that what Tiger does in his own year will stay with Tiger for the next decade. Whatever the Tiger chooses to do now, fate will be kind and flexible, allowing the Tiger to make long-term plans. This is a particularly good time for following romantic inclinations. Marriages and relationships are especially well starred when the bold Tiger hunts in his own year.

The Tiger in the Hare Year: The seeds that Tiger planted in his own year will start to sprout and flourish in the Year of the Hare. In the race of life the Tiger will swiftly move ahead of all others. But a note of caution should be sounded because a boastful, show-off attitude won't help Tigers to win friends and influence people, so it is best if he is a little more modest about his achievements.

The Tiger in the Dragon Year: Tiger and Dragon have much in common, but even so it's important for the Tiger to know his place. After all, this is the Dragon's year and the wiser Tiger will accept this and be content to play second fiddle. In other words, don't rock the boat. As long as he is professional and businesslike, and the Tiger will find a way to prosper in this year!

The Tiger in the Snake Year: This will tend to be a frustrating year for Tiger. Everything seems to slow down as life, like a slug-gish river meanders across a plain. All the Tiger can do is to sit back and go with the flow. Taking a little time out will help Tiger to unravel his fraught nerves, learn to relax a little and to appreci-ate life more fully!

The Tiger in the Horse Year: This will be a very good year for Tiger. All areas of life will improve beyond the Tiger's reasonable expectations. Even though things are going well, it is a wise Tiger who will ignore the urge to take big risks or show-off. This year, the Tiger should work hard and enjoy his good fortune without letting his successes go to his head!

The Tiger in the Goat Year: Tiger's revolutionary zeal will fall out of favor in the Year of the Goat. The Tiger will tend to stand out for all the wrong reasons, leading to misunderstandings and feelings of alienation. In this year it's best if the Tiger sits back and takes note of developments going on around him. Tigers must learn patience and wait until their individualistic style is more in vogue!

The Tiger in the Monkey Year: Fortunes will improve for the Tiger in a year filled with dramatic twists and turns. Revolutionary ideas will become more fashionable putting Tiger back in control. Whatever the creative Tiger can imagine will be achievable during the Monkey Year and it may be that only the Tiger's vision could possibly imagine where it will all lead!

The Tiger in the Rooster Year: The Tiger's social life will receive a boost during this year. Any problems occurring now will tend to be minor and short lived. Even though the practicalities of life are not to the fore in the Rooster Year, Tigers will sort out a lot of petty irritations. It is in the area of romance that Tigers will "burn bright," relationships, both long and short-term will be very fortunate for Tiger in this year!

The Tiger in the Dog Year: The Year of the faithful Dog is auspicious for the Tiger. Revolutionary ideals will once again find favor.

In career terms, the going might be challenging, yet the Tiger will cope with this and even prosper as his innovative thinking will solve problems and increase productivity. In addition, Tigers will still find time to focus on long-term friendships and relationships!

The Tiger in the Pig Year: Tigers will develop a more easy-going nature during happy-go-lucky Year of the Pig. It's inevitable and some standards will drop while the Tiger's finances shrink while other people seem to prosper but this is nothing to worry about. The wiser Tigers will realize that this petty setback is a minor phase of life and will eventually end. Tigers should use this time to experience a little more of life!

The Hare

7

(1939, 1951, 1963, 1975,
1987, 1999, 2011)

The Hare is considered to be the sign of virtue. It represents longevity, high standards and prudence. The legendary Chinese character of the Hare on the Moon is said to be always busy grinding the ingredients of the elixir of immortality with a mortar and pestle. The Buddha is believed to have taken the form of a hare in one of his previous incarnations.

The Virtues of the Hare

Sensitive, refined, tactful, prudent, cultured, creative, considerate, gracious, discreet and long living

The Vices of the Hare

Pedantic, haughty, self-indulgent, hypochondria, judgmental, condescending, self-righteous

The Hare Personality

The Hare is a refined and fastidious creature and his good taste is shared with those born under his sign. Some Hare personalities are quite aloof and snobbish, but that is not a universal characteristic. Hares are often reserved, preferring to stand back from the common throng, but that does not always mean that they consider themselves to be superior. They are good at creating an impression that they are imaginative, self-assured people with cool, emotional detachment. In fact, this is an expression of their highly-strung, sensitive natures. In short, Hare people tend to get very upset by confrontations and dramas unless they cause them, in which case they can quite enjoy the chaos they create.

Hare people often possess great intelligence, interesting looks and a reserve and refinement suggesting an aura of mystery. In addition, the observant Hare is often extremely intuitive, often psychic.

The Hare in Love

There are only two ways that others can react to the Hare person. Either he will be respected and admired, or respected and loathed, but he will always be respected! In relationships it is vital to remember that, although the facade of the Hare is impressive, it conceals a deep sense of inadequacy. A threatened Hare will react to hostility by either raging wildly or even worse, by cutting his opponent to the quick with cold sarcasm and then quickly retreating.

Hares desperately need tenderness, understanding, trust and security within a close relationship. The easily frightened Hare will shy away from brash types but may be wooed by quiet sincerity and persistence.

The Hare is likely to find love will the artistically gifted Goat, the sensitive Pig, and the loyal Dog.

The Horse, Snake, Ox, and Tiger will develop into friends, but for real mutual appreciation try another Hare!

The Hare will sense a threat from the ostentatious Dragon, and his refinement will be appalled by the forthright candor of the Rooster and the overt charm of the Rat.

The Hare Career

With such refined sensibilities it is not surprising that many Hare people are artistically gifted, so any career that involves an expression of personal flair and good taste will find favor with the Hare. Hares would not enjoy the rough and tumble of business life or a career with too much pressure. They prefer to work at their own pace in a methodical manner.

One may find the Hare in such diverse careers as writer, librarian, artist, designer or diplomat. Hares excel at public relations and may also consider the law, becoming an attorney, judge or a court recorder.

The Hare and the Five Elements

The five ancient elements of Chinese tradition will give extra variations to the Hare character.

The Wood Hare (1975)

The Wood Hare personality is conventional, intelligent, quiet and modest. Wood Hares possess a compassionate nature, which often leads them to help others who are less fortunate. If they can accomplish this charity work in an anonymous, or at least an unobtrusive fashion, so much the better. They may excel in the fields of athletics or writing.

The Fire Hare (1987)

Artistic temperament is found in the Fire Hare personality. This Hare is likely to be highly-strung, eccentric in habits, emotional, intuitive bordering on the psychic. The medical professions appeal to some but others are drawn to healing with alternative therapies. Fire Hares are cheerful, popular, and fun loving, devoted to their families. Security is vital in relationships and the same applies to the way they handle finances.

The Earth Hare (1939, 1999)

This is an extremely logical Hare, one who holds to sound common sense in all his dealings. Not very ambitious and generally reliant on someone close who is altogether tougher and more pragmatic. This is an easy-going Hare who wants a quiet, ordinary life. The Earth Hare is careful with money and devoted to conventional family values believing that a sound education is the foundation of the future.

The Metal Hare (1951, 2011)

This Hare is likely to be a connoisseur, a collector, or if one is to be harsh, a hoarder! The Metal type can be considered to be moody, but he actually needs periods of solitude. However, this does not make him a hermit, far from it, the sincerity of the Metal Hare wins him influential friends and allies. Emotionally, this Hare is possessive and in general is very protective of friends and family.

The Water Hare (1963)

The Water Hare is an artistic dreamer. This type is sensitive, romantic, very caring and so emotional that he is easily upset. Unusually for the Hare personality, this type doesn't seem to mind financial insecurity as long as he can express himself creatively. The Water Hare loves to travel and often entertains with imaginative tales of his adventures. This is not an ambitious Hare. He is usually content with what he has.

The Year of the Hare

The Year of the gentle Hare will come as a relief after the turbulence of the Tiger year. Traditionally the Hare Year is thought of as a time of peace and harmony when hostilities should cease and rebuilding should begin. Of course this relatively quiet period will not suit everyone. Those who wish to race ahead with their plans will find this period frustrating. To those who have been stressed then this is a welcome time, notable for an easing of pressure and a return to tranquillity. The charitably minded will do best this year. Those who put the interests of others before their own are likely to do very well even though that is not their intention. This year is also good for family life. It is considered to be excellent for marriage and for increasing the size of the family.

An upturn in the world's financial markets is to be expected in the Year of the prudent Hare so excellent investments and profits are possible. In the creative sphere, innovation in fashion and some masterworks in the arts and media are to be expected.

The Fortunes of the Hare Year by Year

The Hare in the Rat Year: This will be a year filled with peril and pitfalls for any Hare who does not keep his wits about him. There are far too many chances of deception and hidden dangers for the Hare. Senses should be sharpened if Hare is to find his way through the traps and lies of false friends who have but one motive, to part Hare from his hard earned cash!

The Hare in the Ox Year: The Year of the diligent Ox provides plenty of challenges for the Hare as well as teaching some hard lessons. Attention must be paid to the less glamorous aspects of life. Hard work and the mundane practicalities of life will take over now. Even so, the Hare should not dread this year because he will learn much about himself as well as adding to his life experience.

The Hare in the Tiger Year: A year of revolutionary changes is forecast when Hare meets Tiger. It is fortunate that the fierce Tiger is a friend of the Hare and will help him to adapt in this time of upheavals. It is more than likely that the Hare will weather the storms that overwhelm others and eventually profit from this turbulent time!

The Hare in the Hare Year: It is an extremely fortunate time for the Hare during its own Year. Past troubles will be forgotten as Hare looks to the future with a new sense of hope and adventure. Luck will be with the Hare, and although a little risk taking might pay off initially its important to take care of money because there is a possibility that less scrupulous folk may try to take advantage of the Hare's good nature.

The Hare in the Dragon Year: The outgoing exuberance of Dragon will disturb the quiet refinement of Hare. The philosophical Hare will just have to learn to lay low and avoid the turmoil that is a constant feature in the lives of those around him. At least the Hare knows instinctively when it is time to "go to ground" and some discretion as well as some fancy footwork might be in order this year!

The Hare in the Snake Year: This is a great year for the Hare, as he can follow his intellectual nature and take up a course or enter higher education. Although this might lead to criticism and certain problems within friendships, simply because it would be too easy for the Hare to develop a superior attitude, becoming aloof and selfish. Remember that the whole point to the exercise is to pursue a better understanding of the world!

The Hare in the Horse Year: Things will pick up pace for Hare during this year, but the Hare will cope well with this increase in speed and he will deal with all that the world can throw at him. The only source of worry might be the Hare's tendency to involve himself in other people's problems. This would not be a good move so it is best if the Hare attended to his own concerns and developed a certain reserve and emotional distance.

The Hare in the Goat Year: The Goat is a compatible sign to the Hare so this year is likely to be a good one. Even though, in the early months of the year, the money situation could be better Hare will still manage to enjoy the finer things in life and develop new and stimulating friendships. The Hare will seek out the company of like-minded people who will appreciate his refined qualities.

The Hare in the Monkey Year: Life seems to descend into chaos in the year of the chattering Monkey. Other people will constantly change their minds and act in a strange, disconcerting manner. This will prove to be an anxious time for the gentle Hare personality and the best thing that he can do is stand aloof, and if possible, well away from more excitable people. Smarter Hares will hide and use this time to follow more intellectual pursuits.

The Hare in the Rooster Year: The Year of the Rooster is not favorable to the Hare's financial fortunes. It is likely that the cash flow will dry up to a slow trickle and it is too easy for the Hare to fall pray to anxiety. Sudden and unexpected problems will plague him and the best thing for the Hare to do is lie-low and let the world move on without him. The Hare must avoid moneymaking schemes as they could prove to be very costly.

The Hare in the Dog Year: After the worrying experiences of the Rooster Year, the sensitive Hare can be excused if he is still be looking for problems around every corner as the era of the Dog dawns. However, problems this year are unlikely to be external and your own anxiety and paranoia are the only real difficulties facing the Hare. As time passes the Hare will relax as life finally settles down to a more comfortable pace!

The Hare in the Pig Year: The Hare will breathe a sigh of relief as the year of the Pig comes around. Fate will smile upon the Hare now as both romantic and financial good fortune is with him. The welcome injection of extra money will boost the Hare's social life. The Hare might even have a total image-change. The Hare should get out and about to see a little more of the world. Many will meet a new love interest somewhere along the way.

The Dragon

8

(1940, 1952, 1964, 1976,
1988, 2000, 2012)

The Dragon is considered to be the sign of good fortune and has been used as the heraldic emblem of the Chinese emperor and in a more general sense, as that of China itself. This powerful mythic creature symbolizes the inexorable course of destiny and the forces of nature.

The Virtues of the Dragon

Magnanimous, charismatic, principled, accomplished, good hearted, wise

The Vices of the Dragon

Bombastic, dissatisfied, ruthless, demanding, opinionated, ego-centric, willful

The Dragon Personality

A person born in the year of the exhibitionist, enthusiastic and demanding Dragon will be outspoken, versatile, resilient, energetic, stylish and proud. He is lively and will have a natural charisma and never, ever fade into the background or be ignored. The Dragon person is confident. He believes in himself and possesses very high standards, demanding perfection both from himself and from others. This trait is often mistaken for arrogance. However, the Dragon person will always act with good intentions even if his tact is somewhat lacking.

The Dragon in Love

Even though Dragons possess high principles, they have a very individual way of expressing their honorable intentions, especially in affairs of the heart. Their precious moral code may be only moral in their own opinion, and not that of the society that they inhabit. Dragon people often display a promiscuous streak in their nature and are capable of maintaining multiple relationships. Woe betide any lover who is too emotionally dependent or jealous because they will find themselves swiftly, and sometimes ruthlessly, dumped! Having said that, the Dragon will retain the affections of ex-lovers long after the flame of passion has gone out.

Those most romantically compatible with the charismatic Dragon are born under the signs of Monkey and Rat. However both the Rooster and the Snake will both find Dragon charm irresistible.

On a more platonic level, the Dragon person will be happy and intellectually stimulated in the company of the Tiger, Pig, and Goat.

However, neither the Dog nor the Ox will be in sympathy with the exuberant Dragon personality. Ancient tradition has it that "The Dragon flies to the clouds at the sight of the Hare." Two Dragons together will tend to be extremely competitive and quarrel frequently so no there is little chance of happiness with those of your own sign either.

The Dragon Career

Dragon people are lucky, courageous, intelligent and capable. It follows that Dragons are risk-takers who have no patience with the cautious, slow, long-term approach to business matters. Ambition is the great driving force to Dragons and they will not allow anyone else to thwart their plans. They exude authority, which most people will take at face value. They excel in fields where a display of panache and flair are required but if they could develop an attention to detail then ultimate success is assured.

The Dragon and the Five Elements

Each of the five elements of Chinese tradition adds a further level of interpretation to the Dragon character.

The Wood Dragon (1964)

The Wood Dragon is logical, inventive and creative but often eccentric. Although they are ardent lovers and desire admiration, Wood Dragon people are often too independent to settle down and prefer to live alone. A person born in the Wood Dragon year will have a comfortable life style, he will enjoy life and he can look forward to a happy old age.

The Fire Dragon (1976)

The Fire Dragon is competitive, outspoken and argumentative, determined to get his own way! This forthrightness may sound unappealing but it is actually attractive, and like all Dragons, the Fire type possesses considerable charm. One is never bored in the company of this adventurer. However, Fire Dragons tend to be self-absorbed and prone to accidents.

The Earth Dragon (1988)

Earth Dragon just *know* that they are right.... About everything! Infuriatingly, they usually are! To be fair to them, they are truly gifted and outstanding, probably destined to move among influential people. When seeking a mate, they should marry for love for then they achieve great fortune. However should they make the mistake of marrying for status or money then disaster will strike them and their loved-ones.

The Metal Dragon (1940, 2000)

The Metal Dragon loves material wealth and the high life. He may be a little too obsessed by status and he can fall prey to envy. He is blunt and forceful in his opinions but he remains charming. The one truly negative trait ascribed to Metal Dragon personalities is that they are thought to be tight-fisted. In short, they are considered mean!

The Water Dragon (1952, 2012)

The Water Dragon personality is extremely faithful, intelligent and honorable. The arrogance of the Dragon is still evident, and Water Dragons will refuse to be advised in any matter. These Dragons are great readers and they are often very learned. Female Water Dragons are often drawn to psychic or spiritual matters. Water Dragons of both genders are not complete unless they have a soul mate who truly appreciates them.

The Year of the Dragon

The Year of the Dragon is notable for a series of extraordinary events. It begins with a bang, usually with an amazing occurrence, and the end of the year often brings a repeat of the astonishing event that started it. This year is favorable to any who would take a calculated risk. It is favorable to those who think big, and are prepared to work towards their goal. It must be remembered that the Dragon does not favor the idle or those who avoid their responsibilities. Many people will feel that fate has taken a hand in their lives in the Dragon Year.

It is said that in the Year of the Earth Dragon, nature itself will become turbulent, so earthquakes and cataclysms are to be expected. Fortunately we don't have to worry about that until 2048.

The Fortunes of the Dragon Year by Year

The Dragon in the Rat Year: The Rat loves the Dragon so you can expect happiness and appreciation this year. Your love life will bring you joy and security while your domestic situation will be comfortable and contented. The Dragon will be flattered and feted, amused and adored. In fact the only concern is a tendency to be an outrageous spendthrift.

The Dragon in the Ox Year: The traditionalist Ox is no friend to the innovative Dragon so this could be a fairly dismal year. The usual Dragon sparkle is muted and a headlong reliance on luck is not advised. The Dragon must think before acting because, for once, fortune does not favor the bold. In the Ox year the Dragon must grudgingly bide his time for once.

The Dragon in the Tiger Year: The Tiger is the Dragon's friend so this is beneficial to financial fortunes and the life and there is a taste for adventure. The Dragon is likely to achieve great things and he may also be rewarded for a courageous act. However, he must guard against arrogance or being too ready to bask in the limelight or he'll have cause to regret his boastfulness.

The Dragon in the Hare Year: The Dragon is incompatible with the Hare so this is likely to be a boring and difficult year. The Dragon's exuberance and enthusiasm will be unappreciated, and that is a hard thing for the proud Dragon to bear. So he must be prepared to step back, watch his manners and quietly make steady, unassuming progress.

The Dragon in the Dragon Year: This is a "make or break" year that will herald a series of challenges for Dragons. While it is true that there are plenty of opportunities for the Dragon to excel, there are likely to be a lot of hurdles to get over as well. Fortunately, you will be particularly charismatic at this time and your finances should be on the increase too. A Dragon in the Dragon year must now show the world what you're made of and prove that your grandiose ideas are worthwhile.

The Dragon in the Snake Year: The Snake is compatible with the Dragon, so this year should be fortunate. However, the Snake favors those who are subtle, so it will be a wise Dragon who knows when to keep his opinions to himself. You are likely to benefit from other people's mistakes and you may develop a deeper understanding of human foibles and frailties. Try not to be distracted by petty politics and power play.

The Dragon in the Horse Year: Fate takes a hand in the Dragon's affairs this year and abundant good fortune ensures that this is going to be a fast and furious exciting ride. This is a year for adventure and enriching your life experience. Don't allow your good fortune to go to your head and curb any tendency to act in a superior manner to those less fortunate than yourself.

The Dragon in the Goat Year: The inspiring Goat urges the Dragon to express his boundless creativity. Dragons who work in the media, theatre or the arts will do very well, but even those who have more conventional careers will find new talents. Negative influences will leave your life and new companions who appreciate your gifts will be welcomed.

The Dragon in the Monkey Year: The unpredictable Monkey Year could make the Dragon feel insecure. This might be a good thing as it will prevent you from charging ahead regardless into disaster. Don't be too proud to admit to a mistake or change a course of action that you know instinctively to be wrong. On a more positive note, the Monkey adds excitement and variety to the love life.

The Dragon in the Rooster Year: The Rooster is a friend to the Dragon but he demands total candor, especially in relationships.

This could be bad news for the Dragon's love life and make you question your emotional commitments. On the other hand, career and finances will do well ensuring that your personal security is assured long after this year has ended.

The Dragon in the Dog Year: The Dog demands total fidelity and the flighty Dragon will find that this is a difficult time in his love life. The truth is that the Dragon will find it impossible to be selfish and will learn grudgingly to put the interests of others first. He may well benefit in the long run from this selflessness, but it will still create unease in the Dragon character.

The Dragon in the Pig Year: The Pig admires the Dragon so this is a very lucky year with astonishing successes in every sphere of your life. Now you will find the appreciation, not to say adulation that you've sought! However, it would be wise to keep that arrogance in check or you could squander all the goodwill that has been built. A little modesty while you're at the pinnacle of success will gain you a lot of respect.

The Snake

9

(1941, 1953, 1965, 1977,
1989, 2001, 2013)

The Snake is considered to be the sign of wisdom. The Snake is wise, glamorous and cunning, beautiful and elegant. It is important to remember that when dealing with a Snake there is always an underlying hint of a threat.

The Virtues of the Snake

Amiable, honorable, fun-loving, sympathetic, philosophical, fashionable, charitable, intuitive, diplomatic and sexy

The Vices of the Snake

Arrogant, conniving, clinging, pessimistic, ostentatious, faddish, and a very sore loser

The Snake Personality

Those born in the year of the subtle Snake are usually intelligent, decisive, stylish, and eloquent. Easily bored by repetitive activities, Snakes love variety in everything. A lover of stimulating debate, a Snake person will not tolerate idle chatter for long before moving on to something infinitely more interesting. A quick and accurate judge of situations and people, the Snake usually looks beneath the surface and soon has a very good idea of what is going on among the complexities. The Snake person will make a good friend but an unforgiving enemy.

The Snake in Love

The Snake personality is an independent one. Snakes rarely feel the need for other people's approval and regard it as beneath them to take other people's views into account. A Snake's greatest dread would be to become totally dependent on someone else. Secondary to that, to appear foolish or weak would almost be as shameful. So it can be seen that the Snake personality requires a very forgiving partner, one who will appreciate the foibles or an essentially eccentric character. However, the Snake is sexy and sensual so these traits will prove an attractive lure to a prospective mate.

The Snake personality is very seductive and very attractive. Snakes are most suited to the candid Rooster whose insistence on telling the truth will captivate this serpent. Perhaps the Snake doesn't find it necessary to pretend to the Rooster. The diligent Ox is also considered most a compatible lover. The Snake finds his strength very attractive indeed.

Snakes will make friends with those of their own sign as well as winning the appreciation of Rats, Hares, Dragons, Goat, and Dogs.

The overly sentimental Pig will irritate the Snake who will open his jaws wide to devour the poor creature. The Tiger is odious to the Snake. According to traditional Chinese belief, "Should the Snake catch sight of the Tiger, it is as if he were wounded with a knife."

The Snake Career

Snakes are logical and organized workers who possess the patience that is required to acquire many skills. The Snake is capable of swiftly understanding and then competently handling the most complex situations. He will set about his duties in a quiet, controlled manner—preferably operating alone, with little outside interference. In financial terms, Snake people are often very lucky sometimes coming into money through inheritance, divorce settlements, winnings or unexpected strokes of luck.

Professions that best suit the Snake character include politics, public relations, psychologist, entrepreneur, philosopher, archaeologist and astrologer. However any career that involves traveling and a varied range of new activities would suit the Snake well.

The Snake and the Five Elements

The Five elements of oriental tradition also have an influence on those born under the sign of the Snake.

The Wood Snake (1965)

The Wood Snake person often has a difficult start in life. He may suffer early ill health or experience poverty. He is therefore cautious and conscious of personal security right through his life. The Wood Snake has a subtle mind and is fascinated by intrigue and the dark byways of history. This is a very witty Snake who hates crowds and mess. He is vain especially about his hair. In affairs of the heart, the Wood Snake is attractive, seductive and very fickle.

The Fire Snake (1977)

The Fire Snake has a huge personality that is impossible to ignore. He is a dominant force, self-possessed, arrogant and opinionated. Usually found in the company of influential people, this is an extremely ambitious Snake, who may yet regret the choices he has made and the price he has paid to fulfill his desires. In love, the Fire Snake is a little too self-centered for comfort.

The Earth Snake (1989)

The Earth Snake is extremely determined and never loses sight of his long-term goals. He is a hard worker and considered to be fortunate. He is likely to be conservative in his opinions, regarding order and precision as the supreme virtue. Canny and lucky in business matters and property dealings he is likely to become wealthy. However, in love, the Earth Snake person may appear callous, yet he needs a loving and understanding companion.

The Metal Snake (1941, 2001)

A Metal Snake person is extremely talented with unique gifts, yet his eccentricities, lack of firm direction, his pride and capacity for deception can lead to unpopularity. It is too easy for a Metal Snake character to alienate potential allies who would help him. If one can get past the formidable defenses, Metal Snakes will become good and loyal friends, though they are equally likely to become unforgiving and underhanded enemies. Male Metal Snakes are usually attracted to younger women while the female of the species are drawn to influential older men.

The Water Snake (1953, 2013)

The Water Snake personality is fastidious, astute, intelligent and pragmatic. It could be said that Water Snakes have a lateral view of life and a sly, wry sense of humor. Happiest when slithering through the corridors of power, Water Snakes are ambitious, charming and lucky. Not noted for emotional declarations or outbursts, this Snake is an intellectual, and prefers the company of those who are also mentally alert.

The Year of the Snake

The Snake lives in hollows and under stones so in its own year it's no surprise that some of these stones will be overturned. This year casts an eye on many questions and mysteries that haven't seen the light in a very long time. Politicians and national governments will feel the full glare of the serpent's merciless gaze, and we can be sure that the cunning serpent will not rest until every scandal is rooted out and all mysteries revealed.

More generally, the Snake favors those who are patient and subtle, however people who are rash and impetuous will have cause to regret their thoughtless haste.

The Snake is an inventive sign so this is going to be a year for innovations. Remarkable scientific breakthroughs and astonishing discoveries are due at this time. Equally, the stylish elegance of the Snake will find a reflection in the arts and the world of fashion. New trends in fashion, music, film, theatre and TV are very likely.

The Fortunes of the Snake Year by Year

The Snake in the Rat Year: This will be a trying year for Snakes. Sudden changes are likely to play havoc with your emotions and even though the financial outlook is quite good, you could well be left wondering why you bother as you struggle to find enough money to go around! All in all, this is one year when Snakes will feel generally harassed.

The Snake in the Ox Year: The Ox is a fortunate sign for the Snake but even so, the slow plodding pace will be a little wearing. Money worries are likely to occupy your attention at the Chinese New Year and Snakes will wonder when your financial troubles will ease. Take comfort, because the Ox may be slow but he is steady and sure and as his year progresses the Snake will see gradual improvements. It's just a matter of staying cool and keeping your head.

The Snake in the Tiger Year: Life will again pick up pace for Snakes during this year. You slow steady serpents will struggle with this, especially during the early months as foolish accidents cause you to lose face. Just try and go with the flow, because life will move more smoothly the less you struggle!

The Snake in the Hare Year: The year of the stylish Hare will prove a relief to the fraught Snake. The refined pace of life will suit the Snake much better and frustrations will soon ease. At last Snake personalities will feel more confident and will soon find both the time and the money to enjoy life's pleasures. It's a great time to get out more. To see a little more of the world and to do it in style!

The Snake in the Dragon Year: Although this will be a year full of bluster and dramas, the Snake will be thankful that these will tend to happen to other people. This is an ideal time for Snakes to slither off into a hole and avoid these problems. Remember, that no matter how well-intentioned Snakes are they can't take care of everything and they have to get their priorities right. In the Dragon year, self-interest and self-preservation are no bad thing.

The Snake in the Snake Year: Opportunities will come knocking for Snakes during his own year. Fortunately he will be more than ready to make use of them, whatever has been dreamt of in the past will now be made possible if Snakes can find the determination to make it all happen. This is also a good time to pour oil on troubled waters as old arguments will now be forgotten and life will become more peaceful!

The Snake in the Horse Year: Snakes will find the Year of the Horse a rather difficult one to cope with. The usual subtle tactics won't work and it would be best for Snakes to avoid far reaching legal transactions or business dealings because very little will go according to plan. The Snake must try and be honest and open in his dealings because it will be all too easy to have one's motives misunderstood or misrepresented.

The Snake in the Goat Year: If the Snake's motivations were called into question in the Horse year then the opposite applies in the Year of the Goat. Untrustworthy and unscrupulous people might try and worm their way into your life by playing on your emotions. So a wise Snake will be extremely cautious and take extra care. After all, more than money may be lost, and the Snake's ability to trust might be a casualty of this emotionally difficult time.

The Snake in the Monkey Year: Although Snakes enjoy a little intrigue; the chaos of the Monkey Year could cause more confusion than is comfortable. Snakes are likely to spend an enormous amount of time struggling to work out what's really going on. Snakes must make an earnest attempt to not get involved in anything that doesn't affect you directly even if this means lowering your standards to stay out of trouble!

The Snake in the Rooster Year: The Rooster is a friend of the Snake and although there might still be a few problems to iron out, this will be a much better year for Snake people. Plans will move a step closer to becoming reality as new friends and allies will offer practical help and with a bit of luck you might even find new love! All in all, the Rooster Year should provide a boost to the Snake's income and ego.

The Snake in the Dog Year: Snakes tend to fare well in the Year of the faithful Dog. The financial and practical side of your lives will see improvement and it is likely that Snakes will themselves in an exciting new job or running a new and profitable business. One word of caution, remember that life is about more than hard work and worldly success. Snakes should also find some time to enjoy themselves too to combat mounting stress levels.

The Snake in the Pig Year: Some species of snake such as the python are capable of swallowing a pig whole so it's not surprising that Snake personalities will want to consume all the opportunities this year brings immediately. Snakes will feel more in control this year, some might move house or give their old one a make over. Although the picture looks rosy try not to be too greedy and not too impulsive. The only real thing to beware of is the danger of being lead astray by a close friend or lover!

The Horse

10

(1930, 1942, 1954, 1966,
1978, 1990, 2002, 2014)

The Horse is considered the sign of ardor because passions play a big part in this impetuous steed's life. Subsidiary interpretations of the Horse character include a strong possibility of the establishment of a distinguished career. In Chinese tradition, the Horse represents nobility.

The Virtues of the Horse

Productive, warm-hearted, enthusiastic, amusing, industrious, agreeable, sociable, logical, strong minded

The Vices of the Horse

Defiant, unscrupulous, opportunistic, moody, self-serving, unwilling to listen to reason

The Horse Character

Horse personalities are cheerful, independent minded, outgoing, often outspoken and they are usually very popular on account of their immense charm. Easily affected by the moods of others, Horses thrive in the company of lively, cheerful people. They usually rise to the occasion, amusing their audience and inspiring passions with their eloquent words. On the other hand, if the Horse does not receive the appreciation he desires from those around him, then he is likely to become moody, impatient and sarcastic.

The genuine enthusiasm of the Horse personality will easily win friends who will want to confide their deepest secrets to this noble equine. It is here that the basic fault of the Horse character becomes evident. It is a sad truth that the Horse finds it almost impossible to keep tight lipped, especially if the secret is particularly juicy.

The Horse in Love

Horse personalities love to be in love. Often caught up with the thrill of romance, the impulsive Horse is exhilarated by new relationships, sometimes to the point of forgetting existing responsibilities as he happily races into new, tempestuous emotional links. Of course, in youth this trait does lead to some scrapes, so Horses have generally been around the track a few times before they settle down. However, the Horse can be tamed by soothing words, genuine affection, and a demonstration of tenderness.

Those best suited to a long relationship with a spirited Horse are the ever-faithful Dog, the refined and talented Goat, and the courageous Tiger.

The Horse enjoys lively company, so the friendship of Dragons, Snakes, Monkeys, Roosters, and Pigs are most agreeable.

The Horse won't be so comfortable in the company of the opportunistic and devious Rat or the snobbish Hare. The Ox may be too slow and precise for the exuberant Horse, and according to Chinese tradition "The White Horse cannot share a stall with the Black Ox." This means that a Horse person who happens to be born in a year governed by the Metal element should never marry a Water Ox.

The Horse Career

Most Horse personalities possess a strong sense of responsibility and will work very hard on behalf of their families and dependants. Horses are noted for astonishing stamina. Horses can work, party or athletically push their physical boundaries until everyone else has collapsed with exhaustion. Horse people are also clever with their hands, and, being so active, many born under this sign are great travelers. The careers best suited to the Horse include construction work, sports, exploring, geography, actor, artist, dress designer, engineer, sales or advertising.

The Horse and the Five Elements

The five elements of Oriental tradition also have their part to play, adding to the characteristics of the Horse.

The Wood Horse (1954, 2014)

The element Wood adds an affinity to the natural world to the spirited Horse personality. The Wood Horse usually prefers country life to the urban sprawl. He is friendly, sociable, and cooperative, but he may have little time for traditional values and practices. The Wood Horse person is intelligent, freedom loving, with a capacity to recover from adversities.

The Fire Horse (1966)

The Fire Horse is wild. Traditional Chinese thought regards him with dread because this personality is often a little too hot to handle. The Fire Horse can be flamboyant, charismatic, ingenious, and clever, but also rebellious, with volatile moods that make stable relationships difficult. The Fire Horse loves travel and he can be a thrill-seeker.

The Earth Horse (1978)

The Earth Horse is very logical; however, this tends to make him weigh everything up for so long a time that he can be indecisive. Even after thinking things through, he is often left in a morass of confusion and needing the guidance of others. This innate insecurity may be concealed by a tendency to act in a bossy manner. The families of Earth Horse people aren't very helpful so friends frequently take the place of relatives. In youth, this is a wild Horse but this type tends to mature well.

The Metal Horse (1930, 1990)

This is a stubborn self-centered Horse who is noted for restlessness, love of variety and a thrill-seeking nature. Never boring (and indeed fearing boredom), he rarely settles long enough to establish stable relationships, this Horse is nevertheless exciting company. It is fortunate that the Metal Horse character can usually afford to live the good life. This flamboyant Horse loves to show off and actually enjoys shocking others. He isn't afraid of controversy or arguments.

The Water Horse (1942, 2002)

The early life for the Water Horse is likely to have been difficult. He is emotionally very vulnerable and he hates noisy arguments or being surrounded by chaotic lifestyles. It is this trait that will enable him to become very successful. He is very competitive, often a traveler, and physically strong and adventurous. A Water Horse is a great listener and an eloquent, persuasive communicator. His close relationships may cause him problems because he finds it easy to make promises but far more difficult to fulfill them.

The Year of the Horse

This is a year in which those who are enterprising and prepared to work hard towards their goals will do very well indeed. Think of the Horse Year as a bucking bronco who will kick and jump, dart from side to side and generally try to throw its rider. All the rider has to do is hang on. Those that can be flexible and take advantage of every opportunity will prosper, while those who give up at the first hurdle will gain nothing except a few bruises.

Plans that have been made in previous years will now come to fruition, however schemes that are off-the-cuff or not well thought out will toss you from the saddle with no warning.

The Horse year favors those of honest, independent attitudes with a sense of flair. The sense of integrity becomes more important because secrets come out in the Horse Year and revelations are all too common, so scandalous celebrities and dubious politicians had better beware.

The Fortunes of the Horse Year by Year

The Horse in the Rat Year: The year of the cunning Rat is likely to be a trying time for honest and straightforward Horse personalities. All the scheming and deceit is distressing and it could lead to feelings of insecurity and worry. Caution should be a wise Horse's watchword because it would be too easy to be befuddled by fast talkers. A Horse should put his own plans on hold otherwise he'll end up find himself fighting battles on all fronts!

The Horse in the Ox Year: The year of the placid Ox should be a comfortable one for Horses. Being in the company of another grazing animal will tend to make this a better year all around. Although this will mean a lot of hard work, at least Horses will feel like you are getting somewhere and that efforts will eventually be rewarded. On the other hand, the love life may quite turbulent.

The Horse in the Tiger Year: The prospects for a Horse's finances will definitely improve during the Year of the daring Tiger. However it is this very urge to be adventurous that could prove to be the Horse's undoing. Although many opportunities will present themselves, he must care must be taken not to be overconfident or to leap into a situation before all the ramifications are fully understood. The same message applies to prospective relationships.

The Horse in the Hare Year: An excellent year is forecast for Horses as they feel the need to widen horizons and make their mark on the world. Some Horse personalities might take this literally and embark on a career that puts them in the public eye. Even if the Horse does encounter a few green-eyed enemies, he shouldn't worry because he won't be able to put a foot wrong!

The Horse in the Dragon Year: The positive influences of the zodiac continue for fortunate Horse personalities in the year of the exuberant Dragon. Horses will be productive, capable, efficient and successful. The Horse's social life will also prosper and a renewed sense of fun and adventure will add to the excitement.

The only downside is that the Horse's notorious tactlessness might come to the fore so if he can manage not to offend too many people along the way he will have a great year!

The Horse in the Snake Year: The level-headed Horse personality seems to take a vacation in the year of the sensuous Snake. The practicalities of life will tend to be ignored as temptation rears its attractive head again and again. Most Horse personalities will find that resistance is futile – not that they will try very hard. However, it would be wise to at least *try* to stay on the straight and narrow because fantasy is likely to overcome realism this year.

The Horse in the Horse Year: Oddly, Horse personalities do not often enjoy the experience of the Horse Year. It's a case of coming back to reality with a bump and many will find the going quite tough at times. However, even though things will be a struggle, Horse personalities will learn valuable lessons along the way. There are indications of a new life path opening but not quite yet! Hold back on making any life changing decisions until things settle down a little!

The Horse in the Goat Year: After the struggles of the previous year the Year of the Goat will seem much easier. Life will enter a period of relative calm and Horse personalities will notice gradual improvements in both the career area and love life. Many Horse people will consider this to be the perfect time to abandon a nomadic life-style and finally settle down!

The Horse in the Monkey Year: As might be expected the Year of the fickle Monkey is one of novelty and fun for Horse people.

There are plenty of opportunities around if Horses are quick off the starting line and if they can keep up the hectic pace. If the Horse is feeling particularly adventurous then he may opt for a gamble or two. That's not to say that all of them will pay off, but the Horse will add to his store of experience and will probably have a lot of fun along the way.

The Horse in the Rooster Year: The judgmental Rooster demands a little more responsibility from the Horse personality. Sensible decisions are favored, while fickleness and a wayward spirit are not. With this in mind, the Rooster year is particularly favorable for the formation of a committed partnership. It is equally good for large investments such as the purchase of a new home. Horses must be prudent now and plan carefully for the future.

The Horse in the Dog Year: This year, the Horse will not be in the character of a racer, but in a more humble aspect as the hard-working plough horse. The faithful nature of the Dog demands that the Horse puts loyalty to others first, so it would be an unwise Horse who acts in a selfish manner. On the other hand, the Dog is favorable to relationships, and many Horse personalities will now be content to share their feelings.

The Horse in the Pig Year: The equine love of taking risks is severely restricted in the Year of the timid little Pig. This is not the time to give into sudden impulses or take silly chances. There will be far too many complications and variables to take a chance, so a wise Horse will be extra cautious even if his prospects seem to be good. He must plan each step and pay more attention to personal security this year.

The Goat

11

(1931, 1943, 1955, 1967,
1979, 1991, 2003, 2015)

As well as being another animal symbolic of agriculture and fertility, the Goat is also considered to be the sign of *art*. In its youthful form as a lamb, this sign is also an emblem of filial piety. In ancient China, the Goat was a common sacrificial animal, it has therefore come to represent an uncomplaining acceptance of fate.

The Virtues of the Goat

Compassionate, easy-going, gentle, sweet natured, creative, artistic, affectionate, fashionable, dislikes strict discipline

The Vices of the Goat

Overly emotional, pessimistic, insecure, indecisive, overly dependent, troubled love life, erratic mood swings

The Goat Personality

Someone born in the Year of the Goat is likely to be thoughtful and studious but often reserved or even shy. Goat people are kind, good-natured, patient, and reliable. This is a dutiful, hard-working type of person, capable of taking on an enormous workload. However, even though they can cope with the pressure for a while, the Goat must be careful that overworking doesn't make cause stress-related illness. Goat people have artistic, somewhat dreamy minds and a deeply sensitive soul. This sensitivity is so delicate that Goat personalities will evolve a sort of psychological armor by putting a display of apparent indifference. This is an effective disguise, but don't be taken in because no one is softer or more caring than the Goat. Bearing this in mind, it is easy to see that Goat characters loathe confrontations and are easily embarrassed by anything vulgar or brash.

The Goat in Love

Goats are attractive people even when their natural insecurity causes them to doubt this fact. They have a superb sense of style, a natural grace and an attractive, yet unassuming, personality. The best side of the Goat character is found in their caring, loving attitude. Their values are based on a spiritual rather than material plane and they are totally lacking in envy or malice. With these characteristics it is easy to see why the Goat is likely to be in demand and considered to be a worthy mate by so many people.

The talented Goat is particularly drawn to those of a similar creative nature. So it is easy to see that happiness is likely to be found with the Horse, the refined Hare, and the sympathetic Pig.

The Goat's unassuming nature will enhance popularity especially with those born under the signs of the Tiger, Dragon, Snake, Monkey, Rooster, and with other Goats.

Pessimism is a Goat's enemy and internal battles will be fought to maintain a positive frame of mind. Signs who are also prone to negative thinking will not do the Goat any favors. The Ox will be left in the dust by the Goat's imagination, the Dog will plunge him into a pit of gloom, and the Goat will feel totally inadequate with the go-getting Rat.

The Goat Career

The Goat is considered to be a fortunate sign, and people born under this artistic and original sign have the ability to turn a bleak, unpromising situation into a glittering success. Rigid schedules and tiresome routines are to be avoided because the Goat has an easy-going nature and he needs variety in his working life. This is not a particularly ambitious sign and Goat people hate the anxiety of competition so early success is unlikely but once that perfect niche has been found the Goat will find professional happiness.

Goat personalities are often to be found working in the arts, the media, as writers or in professions involving health care. Chinese tradition says that Goat were the treasurers of the ancient courts, and it is true that these people have a deft touch with accountancy and the complexities of tax and bureaucracy.

The Goat and the Five Elements

The five elements of Chinese tradition give extra variations to the Goat's character.

The Wood Goat (1955, 2015)

Fair play and honor are the hallmarks of the Wood Goat. This is a deeply thoughtful person who tends to nostalgic, sentimental, good-humored, and compassionate. However, this type may be too trusting and thus can be taken advantage of by less scrupulous people. On the other hand, there will always be someone around to help the Wood Goat out when he is in need. Whatever gender the Goat happens to be, he will tend to "mother" those he loves.

The Fire Goat (1967)

This is not so much a Goat as a Ram! The Fire Goat is courageous, ready to take the initiative and to defend his territory. The artistic side of this Goat will express itself as a love of drama. However, this type will not be so fortunate with money and he is in danger of mismanaging his affairs. This is probably because the Fire Goat is something of a wishful thinker and daydreamer.

The Earth Goat (1979)

Even though the hard working Earth Goat may be described as neurotic, defensive, and literal, he has many positive traits. He is straightforward, trustworthy and stable with a streak of sensitivity. This is a Goat who will gain prosperity through his own efforts. He is extremely creative and happiest when he can share his tastes with like-minded people. The Earth Goat loathes deceit so he may be too honest for comfort especially within a relationship.

The Metal Goat (1931, 1991)

A Goat person born under the influence of the Metal element has more confidence than most other Goats in the flock and a highly refined artistic sensibility. Even so, the ego is still vulnerable and he can be easily hurt. This type is also moody and can be prone to becoming possessive and jealous. He is clannish, family oriented, and he may avoid social situations among strangers.

The Water Goat (1943, 2003)

A Goat influenced by the Water element is desperate for love and approval and he will do anything to get it! The Water Goat is very sensitive indeed; he hates to upset anyone and will usually be content to following the flock. The unassuming, humble Goat prefers not to attract too much notice. As the Water Goat ages, his shyness fades and he blooms, and will become an excellent communicator, easily loved and admired but still much too modest.

The Year of the Goat

The Year of the Goat is a good one for world peace. The Goat loathes confrontations, so international difficulties are likely to be resolved or at least come to a truce in this period. It is equally likely that philanthropic, humane people will rise to positions of power at this time and they will reform corrupt institutions. Traditionally, the Year of the Goat favors anything that will benefit humanity, so social and medical advances are likely.

The artistic side of the Goat is likely to find expression in radical new fashion trends and mass movements, especially those that promote peace.

The Year of the Goat is a good one in which to marry or to breathe new life into a flagging relationship. If a parting of the ways is contemplated, the outlook is not so good, simply because the family-oriented Goat disapproves of divorce.

The Fortunes of the Goat Year by Year

The Goat in the Rat Year: Money can't fail to be top priority in the Rat year with the Goat's anxiety reaching fever pitch. The important thing is not to take any risks with cash. If a Goat is in doubt whether he can afford something or not, the answer is probably not! There's too much temptation to be resisted, but a wise Goat will hold back because the day of reckoning will surely come.

The Goat in the Ox Year: If a Goat has built up debts in the previous year then this demanding time will see him working hard to pay them off. Those Goat people who resisted temptation can now put their efforts into more productive areas and set some firm foundations for their future. The Ox is not exactly a friend to the poor Goat so fun is thin on the ground, but at least the Goat will learn some valuable lessons.

The Goat in the Tiger Year: The year of the demanding, arrogant, and adventurous Tiger could be a difficult one for the Goat's anxiety levels. This is a complex time, and the Goat will need his wits about him. There will be too many ups and downs for him to feel secure. This is a time when a wise Goat will be more unassuming than usual, staying in the background and avoiding fuss.

The Goat in the Hare Year: The refined Hare is compatible with the Goat so there is an injection of fun and laughter this year. The Goat's social graces will be enhanced and taste and artistry will be appreciated. All of this adds up to a time when the Goat will be the person to know. The Goat will make new and influential friends. In financial terms, this year is mediocre, but that is more than made up for by the boost to the Goat's ego and popularity.

The Goat in the Dragon Year: The beginning of this year will be excellent for the Goat. The Goat loves flair and style and the Dragon has an extraordinary amount of it. The Goat imagination will be stimulated and he will be happier and more carefree. The last quarter of the Dragon year might present some minor financial worries so a wise Goat should always save for a rainy day.

The Goat in the Snake Year: Anything that requires talent and flair is favored in the Snake Year, so the creative Goat should be extremely happy at this time. Goats will be appreciated for their fine qualities and talents so any feelings of insecurity or inadequacy will be banished. The Goat will also be very persuasive, and he will be able to talk his way to advantage. Romantically speaking, this is one of the Goat's best years, for love affairs will flourish under the influence of the sensuous snake.

The Goat in the Horse Year: A sense of safety is welcome to the Goat as the Horse year brings some material security. The Goat's knack of creative thinking will make his life much easier. Originality will be appreciated and applauded, and Goat will gain a great deal of respect for the inventive solutions that he comes up with. Travel is well starred in this year.

The Goat in the Goat Year: All the Goat's efforts over the past twelve years will be rewarded when he enters his own time period. The Goat can be himself, free from the complaints, demands and criticisms of others. The more usual anxieties and insecurities will be muted if not forgotten now and this in alone will add to personal charisma. In this year the Goat will gain the confidence to make far reaching, life changing decisions.

The Goat in the Monkey Year: It is impossible to be bored in the Year of the Monkey, and for the Goat, that's likely to be the best thing one could say about it! There is an old Chinese curse that goes, "May you live in interesting times" and these times will be too interesting for comfort for a sensitive Goat. It would be foolish in the extreme for him to take risks or to be too trusting in the unpredictable, ever-changing scenarios that this year will bring.

The Goat in the Roster Year: The Goat's overdeveloped sensitivity could be quite battered by the outspoken candor of the Rooster. The Goat's delicate ego will be devastated if he doesn't keep a low profile this year. It is too easy to be discouraged and to believe that everything is too difficult and beyond his capabilities. This is not so, because while this will be a challenging time, a persistent Goat will get through and come out as a stronger person.

The Goat in the Dog Year: This is a likely to be a year that is notable for self-denial and austerity. I doubt that there is a single Goat that will enjoy that experience. The Goat's need for reassurance may be ignored now simply because other people are too busy with their own concerns to be overly sympathetic to the Goat's sensitivities. A wise Goat will forget his own needs for a while and find a new purpose in helping others in a charitable venture of some kind.

The Goat in the Pig Year: The friendly and sensitive Pig signals a time that is conducive to the Goat's creative nature. It is also good news because the Goat will be able to indulge his taste for luxury. Others will appreciate the talented and imaginative Goat in this compatible year. This is a time when good fortune will find the Goat, but even so it is important the he recognize his limits. So as long as he doesn't push his luck and as long as he moderates his demands, the Goat will do very well indeed.

The Monkey

12

(1932, 1944, 1956, 1968,
1980, 1992, 2004, 2016)

The Monkey is traditionally called the sign of fantasy. Mischievous, resourceful, and intelligent, the Monkey is thought of as the likeable trickster. The familiar—"hear no evil, see no evil and speak no evil"—is of Japanese origin.

The Virtues of the Monkey

Lively, complex, humorous, agile, diplomatic, charming, flexible, excellent memory, resistant to insults, competitive

The Vices of the Monkey

Dishonest, lacking respect, jealous, prone to temptation, restless

The Monkey Personality

Fast thinking, witty, and exciting, Monkeys yearn for a life of constant variety, filled with new and stimulating people. The Monkey's ever-active mind means that he is quickly bored and he loathes the company of boring people. Monkey characters are often very intuitive and quick to catch on to new ideas. Highly intuitive, their unconscious minds operate independently of their conscious thoughts. They are quick to answer any question and they can think about several things at once. Monkeys also possess a quick and ready wit. This can express itself as withering sarcasm, which is one of the Monkey's less appealing features.

The Monkey in Love

Monkeys are attracted to the excitement of being in love. They are in love with love, and just like the idea of being in an ardent romance. It is very likely that those born under this sign experience a lively love life with any number of partners. Potential mates are drawn to the Monkey character by their charm, good humor, openness, and curiosity about the world. In a relationship, the Monkey can be unpredictable or even childish, but it just adds to the excitement and variety. The person who embarks on a long-term relationship with a Monkey must be open-minded and very tolerant. Once trust is gained the Monkey will prove to be a supportive, if unconventional, partner. Even when a relationship ends, Monkeys are very good at retaining the friendship and affection of former lovers.

The Monkey is particularly compatible with those born under the signs of the audacious Rat and the glamorous Dragon.

Monkey will dazzle and make friends easily with those born under the influence of the Dog, the Goat, and the Hare.

The Monkey's sense of humor does not impress the Snake, the Pig, or the Tiger.

The Monkey Career

The versatility and quick-wittedness of the Monkey makes him suitable for a wide variety of jobs; however the Monkey can resent those in positions of authority and they lack the kind of deference that employers tend to expect. Monkey personalities do not gravitate to work in large organizations; by nature, they are far more self reliant and self motivated. The Monkey is capable of hard work as long as he can set his own goals, which he will achieve at his own swift pace. The Monkey is unconventional and creative, and tends to be drawn to careers in the media, public relations, design, and the arts. Some Monkeys take to supervisory roles or become skilled craftsmen, surveyors, and planners.

The Monkey and the Five Elements

Each of the five elements has an influence on the complex Monkey character and adds to the interpretation of the sign.

The Wood Monkey (1944, 2004)

The element of Wood enables the Monkey to achieve stability and success, but only after he gets his restlessness and desire for excitement out of his system. The Wood Monkey personality eventually develops into a street-wise, canny, and shrewd individual who is rarely afraid of anything. Wood Monkeys need firm guidance from a partner, but they will spend a lot of time looking, and lot of time being disappointed. A marriage later in life will be more successful than a early, impulsive partnership.

The Fire Monkey (1956, 2016)

The fiery type of Monkey personality is extremely imaginative, active, and energetic. He can usually be detected by his habit of constantly gesticulating. This is a bold Monkey who is bossy. To be fair, he is a natural leader who can motivate all those around him; however, he can be prone to rashness and will have cause to regret his impulsive actions. He is stubborn and opinionated, constantly right (in his own opinion), very competitive, and prone to unfounded suspicions.

The Earth Monkey (1968)

The Earth Monkey is the most calm and quiet personality of all those born under this sign. He is generous and protective to those that he loves but totally unfeeling and cold to the needs of people at distance from him. In common with other Monkey types, he is mentally agile and knowledgeable – and he quietly but insistently demands that all around him appreciate the fact. He can, like other Monkeys, be roguish and charming, imaginative and clever. If he applies his talents to one endeavor at a time without being distracted then he will be a great success.

The Metal Monkey (1980)

Although the Metal element often gives an outwardly cool, sophisticated, and independent image, the reality is that this Monkey is passionate, possessive, ambitious, creative, and hard working. He will do things his own way and he hates to be advised or directed in any way (he will interpret this as nagging). Creative and intelligent, but a little too conscious of his own image and far too superior for his own good, the Metal Monkey has a strong belief system and he is a profound thinker.

The Water Monkey (1932, 1992)

The Watery nature of this chattering Monkey ensures that he is a charming diplomat and superb negotiator. It is not surprising to find this Monkey in the role of go-between, as an agent, or business representative. This is a shrewd, self-willed, capable and attractive character, bold, eloquent, and stylish. Extremely curious by nature, this type will travel extensively and make influential friends on every continent. Water Monkeys usually tend to marry into money and position, and develop a good relationship with in-laws. On the other hand, Water Monkeys are easily offended, and they mask their insecurities by a barrage of charming words.

The Year of the Monkey

In the Year of the Monkey, the world is ready for everything that is novel, unusual, and the downright eccentric. Ideas that would not have been given an airing in previous years will now be joyfully considered. The Monkey Year is not the best one in which to make long-term plans. The very nature of the Monkey is unpredictable so the best-laid plans will go awry—often before they've even started. In this year, adaptability is the key to success because the wheel of fortune is spinning wildly. Quick profits can be swiftly made but also swiftly lost. Nervous types would be well advised to keep their heads down and not take chances, while the rasher, more enterprising types take all the risks. Romantic inclinations fare better, but even this area will be subject to erratic variations. Those who are flirtatious will have a marvelous time, but those looking to settle down will not fare as well.

The Fortunes of the Monkey Year by Year

The Monkey in the Rat Year: The Rat and the Monkey are compatible signs, so this should be a fortunate year for all Monkey personalities. If Monkeys have felt that they were missing out on the big breaks in previous years, the time of the Rat will be very welcome indeed and it will provide opportunities very swiftly. Finances are favored as indeed is a Monkey's love life. All in all, this is a positive and progressive year.

The Monkey in the Ox Year: The Ox approves of hard work and diligent effort. Although the Monkey *is* capable of sustained effort, they have a hard time sticking to the rules. Even though opportunities will come, the Monkey is unlikely to feel too enthusiastic about them. Most Monkeys will find the Ox Year somewhat dull. However, it does provide the chance to learn a few new skills that will be useful in the upcoming Tiger Year.

The Monkey in the Tiger Year: Even though in personal terms the Monkey and Tiger don't get on, this year should provide some unexpected good luck. The only danger is that a Monkey might take his luck for granted and become complacent and lazy. The clever Monkey will be much in demand as an advisor at this time.

The Monkey in the Hare Year: Happiness is likely to be found in the compatible Year of the Hare. There is a chance to relax and allow all tensions to fade away, and the Monkey will feel more at ease. This is also a chance to reassess, consolidate and to realize that the Monkey has reached a reasonably good position. Romance should flourish and the Monkey's influence grow. This is a very good time to ask for favors.

The Monkey in the Dragon Year: As long as the ever-curious Monkey is prepared to put some effort into improving his education, the Year of the dazzling Dragon should be a good one. This is a time to express ambition and to extend one's experience. Travel to distant lands in order to broaden knowledge is worth doing. However, this is also likely to be an expensive year so Monkeys should be cautious in the use of their resources.

The Monkey in the Snake Year: A Monkey had better be nimble in the Year of the Snake to avoid being caught in its treacherous coils. There are a lot of dangers in this year and a wise Monkey should curb his chattering avoid making enemies or talking himself into trouble. The love life especially is prone to serious complications if the Monkey is not very careful.

The Monkey in the Horse Year: Just as the Snake year encouraged a low profile, the Horse year is another in which caution should be the Monkey's watchword. Individualism is not encouraged at this time and the Monkey may feel constricted by rules and regulations. The financial situation is not promising, so the Monkey must take extra care in dealing with assets and debts.

The Monkey in the Goat Year: The Goat Year arrives with a sigh of relief because it gives Monkeys a chance to sort out their lives and put the difficulties of the past behind them. A creative approach is finally appreciated, and the Monkey will feel more content as he swiftly solves his problems one by one. If the Monkey is mindful of past errors then he is assured of prosperity. By the end of the year, the Monkey should be fairly well off but he should not flaunt his good fortune.

The Monkey in the Monkey Year: In his own year the Monkey reveals his true nature. His curiosity is boundless, his chattering constant and his capacity to handle the most complex issues is staggering. Thoughts of duty and responsibility are cast aside as the Monkey sets out with one aim in mind, which is to enjoy himself. Even though it's probably the last thing on a Monkey's mind, any enterprise started this year is likely to be a roaring success.

The Monkey in the Rooster Year: As long as a Monkey does not believe all he hears in the Year of the Rooster, all will be well. It's a good idea to develop a slight sense of suspicion, to question assumptions and to be a little wary. This is also a time when a Monkey should weigh up the relative importance of friends and associates and treat them accordingly. It would also be a good idea to pay a little more attention to family matters.

The Monkey in the Dog Year: The Year of the Dog is likely to be a dismal one for Monkey personalities. The fun seems to have drained from life as responsibilities and financial anxieties occupy more and more of a Monkey's time. Relationships bring problems because everybody seems worn down by worry and is too preoccupied to pay much attention to a Monkey's concerns. The best trait a Monkey possesses is his resilience and the determination to get through this trying year.

The Monkey in the Pig Year: The green-eyed monster of envy could become an unattractive addition to a Monkey's personality this year, as everyone else seems to be doing well while the Monkey is left behind. This is not true of course but it will be easy to feel that way. The fortunate Year of the Rat will come in after this dull year, so a wise Monkey will knuckle down to work and plan for a time when luck will smile on him again.

The Rooster

(1933, 1945, 1957, 1969, 1981, 1993, 2005, 2017)

13

The Rooster is considered to be the sign of candor and the Rooster symbol is regarded as a potent charm to ward off evil. Chinese tradition holds that the Rooster is endowed with five "virtues": an intelligent mind, shown by his crown; a martial spirit, revealed by his spurs; courage that never backs down from a fight; benevolence because he cares for the hens; and finally, reliability because he always crows at sunrise.

The Virtues of the Rooster

Intelligent, perceptive, honest, excellent memory, alert, organized, generous, attractive, a confident performer

The Vices of the Rooster

Boastful, show-off, opinionated, critical, misunderstood

The Rooster Personality

Those born under the sign of the Rooster have an exhibitionist streak. In Chinese tradition, Roosters were thought to be military types, probably because they like impressive dress uniforms, medals, and banners. Today there are disproportionate amount of Roosters in the media, where they can show off and get paid for it! Even if a Rooster is not in the public eye, he likes to be in the spotlight. His impeccable grooming and individual sense of style often characterize a Rooster. Many will criticize the Rooster for his flamboyance and carefree manner, but this may mask well-concealed shyness. Rooster personalities are independent, surprisingly sensitive, wise, compassionate, and brave. They never shirk duty, they are confident in their own judgments, and they can be straightforward to the point of being unintentionally insulting.

The Rooster in Love

The Rooster is a charmer although many will consider his manner brash and forward. There will be many romantic opportunities in his life and it will be a rare Rooster who does not have a harem of "hens" in his background. Boredom is the Rooster's great enemy, so he is likely to move on if a partner becomes too predictable. The Rooster's essential independence keeps him on the move, at least in early adult life, but this rule is a one-way street: the Rooster has a jealous streak, which he tries to keep well hidden. The female Rooster is usually far more practical than the male, and she is far more impressed by old-fashioned responsibility.

If all this makes the Rooster sound fickle, this is not the case. Indeed, although the Rooster may go to great lengths to give that impression, he is actually capable of deep commitment to an interesting and responsible partner. The necessary stability in close relationships is likely to be found with those born under the signs of the Snake, the Ox, and the Dragon.

The Rooster's sense of style wins appreciation from Tigers, Horses, Goat, Monkeys, and Pigs.

The truthful and straightforward Rooster will hate the snobbery of the Hare and the opportunism of the Rat. Tradition holds that two Roosters cannot share a house in harmony and that "The Cock sheds tears at the sight of the Dog."

The Rooster Career

Roosters are logical thinkers but hate to be pressured or forced into decisions. Their independent streak leads them to prefer working alone at their own pace. This will lead to great productivity, and they can find creative, workable solutions to problems. Needless to say, many Roosters are suited to self-employment. If a Rooster is micro-managed by others he will feel trapped and become overly self-critical. This scenario can lead to depression.

The Rooster is capable of great individual success and can make a lot of money. However, he is liable to spend it as quickly as it accumulates.

Roosters are particularly suited to the media, public relations, commercial sales, and politics. Many become authors, entertainers, and beauticians.

The Rooster and the Five Elements

The five elements of Chinese tradition also have a bearing on the Rooster personality.

The Wood Rooster (1945, 2005)

The Wood Rooster is an optimist even when his chances seem slim. This Rooster is very demanding but fair, decent, and honest. The Wood element makes the Rooster very passionate, not just in an amorous sense (although he will be very ardent) but also in terms of his pet projects. This Rooster is so communicative that he can talk his way into anything.

The Fire Rooster (1957, 2017)

The intense, talented, persevering, excitable, and self-motivated Fire Rooster is destined for the top! This independent-minded Rooster is going to be noticed, he is a natural leader who will easily attract followers whether he intends to or not. His charm ensures that he will make many friends from different walks of life. This Rooster's financial fortunes will increase with the years.

The Earth Rooster (1969)

The Earth Rooster is quick on the uptake and his thinking is systematic and analytical. He is an excellent organizer and better than most Roosters when it comes to controlling his money. The Earth Rooster can be prone to mood swings and also very opinionated. This type of Rooster desperately needs emotional security, so he may marry young.

The Metal Rooster (1981)

The addition of Metal will tend to make this Rooster more abrasive than other types. Metal Roosters are very idealistic, hardworking and determined. However they have notoriously sharp tongues and are considered difficult and moody. If ever a spokesman were needed, the Metal Rooster is the perfect candidate. He is capable of tying his opposition in knots with his skilled and eloquent arguments spiced with some devastating observations. Also, there is no chance of him giving up until he has won.

The Water Rooster (1933, 1993)

The Water Rooster is undoubtedly the great communicator. He simply loves to talk, to gossip and to share any piece of information that comes his way. Indiscretion is this Rooster's middle name. He is at home with any form of communication; writing, computing, and debate. He is organized and persuasive. The Water Rooster has refined taste and loves art and music.

The Year of the Rooster

The confidence of the Rooster should be infectious this year. This is a time when it is right to accept challenges and push the boundaries a little. Like his friend the Monkey, the Rooster is fond of innovation, so this year provides a chance to air ideas that are unusual, unorthodox, and even outrageous. There will be a renewed interest in these strange ideas even if they were previously rejected.

The Year of the Rooster is good news for anyone who wishes to advance at work, achieve a higher status in society and achieve prominence in any creative field. The Rooster brings a sense of order and organization, so where there was chaos a new era will be established. This will be a new set of workable rules, but in affairs of the heart, some partnerships will be put under strain. This is probably because one partner starts to assert a more independent attitude and the terms of the relationship suddenly change.

The Fortunes of the Rooster Year by Year

The Rooster in the Rat Year: This is not the best year for the Rooster and he should restrain any impulse to take risks even if the chances seem on the surface to be very good. Even if Roosters make profits it is doubtful that they will be able to keep them for long. The only way that a Rooster will prosper this year is if he is sensible, if he plans his moves carefully, makes sensible decisions and errs on the side of caution.

The Rooster in the Ox Year: The Ox is a compatible sign so the Rooster will be happier this year. Although the Ox period calls for hard work and favors must be earned, the Rooster's plans will not be obstructed – indeed, many opportunities are bound to come a Rooster's way. Common sense is in fashion this year, so as long as a Rooster does not allow his heart to rule his head all will be well.

The Rooster in the Tiger Year: This will be an exhausting year. Even though Roosters like action, the hectic pace and revolutionary fervor that is in the air will be enough even to wear out the most energetic fowl. Many Roosters will soon have enough of the party and wish to retire in seclusion, but their pride won't allow that, so it's a matter of soldiering right on until the end is achieved.

The Rooster in the Hare Year: Even though the Rooster and the Hare don't really get on, the calmer atmosphere should soothe the nerves. This is not a year for the Rooster to puff up his feathers. He should stick to whatever is familiar and be content with small successes. Practical matters will go well even if they are unspectacular. Romantic inclinations are likely to be unsatisfying.

The Rooster in the Dragon Year: At last there is a chance for the Rooster to show off in the year of the flamboyant Dragon. In fact, the Rooster should make quite and impression and receive a lot of approval. This is a good time to begin anything new. It is excellent for establishing a lasting relationship, marrying or opening a business.

The Rooster in the Snake Year: Good fortune continues into the Year of the Snake. The Rooster and Snake are compatible so romance is well starred. The confidence of the Rooster personality will win favor and it will be permissible for Roosters to be self-assertive and draw attention to their accomplishments. This is bound to create some envy, but Roosters will be so happy that they simply won't care.

The Rooster in the Horse Year: Roosters have a right to feel optimistic in the Horse Year even if there are a few financial hurdles in their path. Hard work is required to solve the problem so it's a good thing that Roosters are not idle. A wise Rooster will look after his health now, ditch some bad habits, eat sensibly and exercise more.

The Rooster in the Goat Year: There are far too many mysteries for Rooster to sleep soundly in the confusing Year of the Goat. Small matters seem to expand into problems of staggering size and too much energy will be expended on trifling details. A Rooster should try to control his anxiety levels and not be too self-critical.

The Rooster in the Monkey Year: This is a chaotic year so the Rooster's instinctive desire for order is bound to be offended. It should dawn on the most obsessive of Roosters that no amount of careful planning is going to make the slightest difference because this is a time when fortunes can change in an instant. As long as a Rooster is adaptable then all will be well. Just go with the flow and don't make a fuss.

The Rooster in the Rooster Year: the Rooster can enjoy himself in his own year. While he is having a good time, he can also plan his next moves and get things started with the confidence that he will ultimately succeed. His bank account may be a little stretched; yet his capacity for hard work will ensure he will soon make up any losses. All the Rooster traits will find appreciation now so he should display his feathers and crow.

The Rooster in the Dog Year: In contrast to his own year, the Rooster is likely to find the Year of the Dog rather dull. It seems that the entire period consists of unrelenting effort with very little reward. Roosters will also be in demand by everyone, sometimes for weird reasons and usually at most inconvenient of moments.

The Rooster in the Pig Year: The Rooster will find his tolerance tested time and again in the Pig Year. He knows instinctively that effort is required to gain anything worthwhile so when things come along too quickly and easily, an element of skepticism and distrust gnaw at the edges of the Rooster's mind. It may be that he is being too suspicious, but it is hard for him to know exactly what is going on. The Rooster will have to wait to find out if the promise of the Pig year will be fulfilled.

The Dog

14

(1934, 1946, 1958, 1970,
1982, 1994, 2006, 2018)

The Dog is valued for its fidelity and is considered to be the sign of wisdom and loyalty. Pekingese dogs were held in such high regard that ownership was confined to the Imperial household. The so called Buddhist lion is actually a palace dog. Statues of these watchful beasts were set up at temple entrances as symbolic protectors.

The Virtues of the Dog

The Dog is moral and has high standards of behavior. He is warm natured and respected with a strong sense of justice. He is a good listener and faithful friend and he is able to spot hidden dangers.

The Vices of the Dog

Anxious, pessimistic, often hot headed, and too critical of love partners

The Dog Personality

Those born under the sign of the Dog have an honest and courageous nature. They are natural crusaders, ready to fight for a worthy cause and to defend their friends and family to the last breath. Dogs easily empathize with the feelings of others and identify with other people's causes and ideals. There is a strong sense of justice here and a Dog person will quickly become offended if he feels that someone else is being taken advantage of or beaten down. This trait is very evident to other people, and they will repay the Dog's loyalty with respect and trust. It is a very rare Dog who will break a promise or betray a confidence.

It is probably because Dog personalities have such a high sense of moral values that they can become hypercritical both of their own behavior and that of others. The strong sense of duty also obliges them to point out other's weaknesses and failing with alarming regularity.

The Dog in Love

Although the Dog is not the most glamorous sign in the Chinese zodiac, people born under the influence of this faithful animal will be very attractive, not least because they are good listeners and they are extremely loyal. However, it will take a lot of coaxing to persuade this canine to reveal his inner feelings because he is wary of burdening others with his anxieties. Dog people need a lot of encouragement and reassurance, so they enjoy the company of a more confident and adventurous partner. A person with a turbulent spirit would be hateful to the Dog who prefers a more reliable and less emotionally intense mate. In romance, the Dog prefers to start with a friendship and allow it to grow, because he hates to be rushed into anything. When a relationship has been established, a Dog must try to control his negative imaginings and not be over-sensitive to his partner's incidental remarks.

The faithful Dog will be happy with the adventurous spirits of the Tiger and Horse as well as with the refinement of the Hare.

The Dog's innate kindness and fidelity are appreciated by the Rat, the Snake, the Monkey, the Pig and, of course, other Dogs.

The Ox will add to the Dog's neurosis and plunge him into a pit of gloom. The Goat has a knack of making the Dog feel inferior, while the strutting Rooster will get on the Dog's nerves. Worst of all, the Dragon's excessive enthusiasms will worry the Dog immensely.

The Dog Career

This is above all a responsible and trustworthy sign, so Dogs will often be found in positions of authority and in possession of sensitive information, which they divulge to no one. The Dog is happiest when his role is clearly defined and his responsibilities are clearly understood by everyone. Dog personalities tend to avoid competitive, aggressive professions and prefer to work as part of a team in a steady, controlled and productive manner. Once a Dog has made a commitment to a project, a course of action or a career path, he will follow it with a conscientious attention to detail and determination in order to make it as much of a success as he possibly can.

Dog personalities are particularly suited to a career in teaching, law, social work, as a doctor, nurse, counselor, campaigner or as a member of the clergy.

The Dog and the Five Elements

The five elements of Chinese tradition add another set of interpretations to the trustworthy Dog personality.

The Wood Dog (1934, 1994)

The genuinely popular, generous and amiable Wood Dogs are certainly house-trained. Very domestic and family oriented they are often experts at do-it-yourself, decorating, and gardening. They derive spiritual strength from their families. Like other types of Dog personality they tend to be honest, considerate and cooperative. According to Chinese tradition, Wood Dogs must be on their guard against strangers and take precautions against theft.

The Fire Dog (1946, 2006)

The addition of the Fire element ensures that this Dog possesses a flair for the dramatic. The Fire Dog tends to be lucky, and he has the ability to make his mark in the world. He is charming, is more adventurous than most other Dog types and he is scrupulously honest. This Dog will have a good reputation and he will be protective his family. More independent that other canines and occasionally rebellious, the Fire Dog enjoys travel and novelty.

The Earth Dog (1958, 2018)

The Earth Dog is an idealist. He is efficient in everything that he does and is respected for his wise and impartial advice. This Dog is methodical and is an excellent organizer of his own affairs and of the activities of others. He may be quite secretive and a persistent worker, often wearing himself out because he never seems to feel the need to take a rest. Periodic financial problems are a recurring feature in the life of the Earth Dog because, despite his natural caution, there is a spendthrift tendency.

The Metal Dog (1970)

The idealistic Dog nature reaches an extreme when combined with the Metal element. The Metal Dog has a dominant personality and is most often found in a position of prominence and authority. Some Metal Dogs are quite tyrannical and very touchy, constantly on the lookout for people or things to be offended by. As usual, this Dog is devoted to his family and he can be a faithful friend. A Metal Dog person is at his best when crusading for a worthwhile cause.

The Water Dog (1982)

The Water Dog personality will make friends easily because he is very attractive, amusing, charming and sympathetic. He is a very good listener indeed and his intuitive understanding of human nature will help him to empathize with others. He loves travel, meeting new people and doing fascinating things. The Water Dog is too restless to settle down in early life but later he will adore his family. Water Dogs easily make influential friends.

The Year of the Dog

The ever-vigilant Dog sounds a warning of danger in this year. It is a timely reminder that one should ensure the security of one's home and possessions. This note of caution will apply to taking gambles too. The sign of the Dog is cautious by nature and he warns against taking too much on trust or going too far out on a limb. The time of brash self-confidence has gone, so this is a time to be extremely sensible. Finances should be invested in something reliable, solid—and let's face it, boring! No resources should be risked on vague promises or apparently spectacular schemes which are literally too good to be true. The Dog year is good news for relationships and a marriage in this year will ensure a lifetime's devotion and fidelity.

The Fortunes of the Dog Year by Year

The Dog in the Rat Year: The Year of the Rat is one of overt materialism and this may offend the Dog's finer feelings. Even though Dogs will observe a lot of injustice in this period it will be difficult to do anything about it, so a wise canine will bide his time. The Dog isn't too happy in the Rat race and will be more content if he can get as far from it as possible.

The Dog in the Ox Year: The all-embracing concentration of practicality that an Ox Year demands has little attraction for the idealistic Dog. Any crusading zeal or revolutionary fervor will be out of fashion for a while, so it would be best for the Dog to toe the line, fit in as much as possible and not be too disruptive.

The Dog in the Tiger Year: This should be a more comfortable period for the Dog because the Tiger will welcome the Dog's revolutionary zeal. The Dog and the Tiger often think alike, and the Dog will be happy, bounding away and enjoying the fast and furious pace of events. The Dog's self-esteem will grow and victory is assured in any conflict. However, the Dog will be more gullible than usual so he should be careful whom he believes and not allow himself to led astray by wishful thinking.

The Dog in the Hare Year: The Hare flees from the Dog and it is usual for the beginning of the Hare Year to be a compete waste of time. There's far too much chasing around and pursuing something that is impossible to catch. A wise Dog will tell himself not to be so excitable and that he must develop a calmer, more philosophical attitude. The Dog's advice will be much in demand, and as the Hare year progresses, romance is favored.

The Dog in the Dragon Year: The Dog had better be prepared to take second place in the Year of the Dragon. It's a time of reassessment and learning, and it would be a good idea for the Dog to accept good advice. Every experience in the Dragon Year will add to the Dog's knowledge and he will get his chance to apply this new wisdom in the future.

The Dog in the Snake Year: The sly Snake is a disturbing influence to the loyal Dog. There are too many upheavals for comfort and the number of intrigues and deceptions will add to the Dog's anxieties. To achieve anything worthwhile this year, the Dog must apply the lessons he has learned and be more assertive. However, it is important that the Dog maintains his integrity and refuses to be drawn into any dodgy dealings.

The Dog in the Horse Year: The Year of the Horse is likely to be filled with minor problems, and this fact alone will keep a Dog on his toes. As long as a Dog personality can maintain his self-confidence and keep to his course then all will be well. However, if he allows his doubts to overcome him he will not achieve success. Even though this is likely to be an anxious time, the Dog's material fortunes should slowly improve.

The Dog in the Goat Year: The Year of the Goat is good news for the Dog's amorous prospects and it is also favorable for any artistic and creative interests. That's the good news! However, Dogs will still be prone to anxieties especially concerning money. It is certain that the Dog will achieve considerable triumphs this year but even victories will cause more worry. Dogs are worriers!

The Dog in the Monkey Year: Fortune favors the brave in the Monkey Year and those Dogs who can overcome their innate caution and take a small gamble will prosper. It's a good year for travel, expanding personal horizons and in the romantic area. Any sector of a Dog's life that has been unsatisfactory will be boosted by an unexpected stroke of luck.

The Dog in the Rooster Year: This year is likely to represent a lesson in reality. The Dog's lofty idealism must take second place when harsh practicalities need to be addressed. This is not to say that he will lose his basic values, but rather that he will have to bow to the prevailing necessities and get down to the nitty-gritty.

The Dog in the Dog Year: In his own year the Dog will be gratified that many of his ideals will be appreciated and put into practice. Dogs will meet with good fortune and others will appreciate their finer qualities. At last, the world will be ready to hear the Dog's views and to act on them. Dog personalities will be praised and although it is not the Dog's nature to believe flattery, he can at least allow himself a few moments of self-congratulation.

The Dog in the Pig Year: The pressure eases in the Year of the Pig, and although canines don't usually allow themselves any downtime, the happy-go-lucky Pig year might force him to do just that. This period provides an antidote to stress, and even Dogs will have to admit that they could do with a little bit more fun. This is a great opportunity to enhance the more cultural, poetic side of the Dog's personality.

The Pig

15

(1935, 1947, 1959, 1971,
1983, 1995, 2007, 2019)

The Pig is considered to be the sign of honesty. It represents wealth, family fortune and abundant possessions. The domestic pig is therefore considered to be a good omen in China, especially when it is covered in mud. If a traveling man should spot a pig on his left hand side, it is said to be a sure indication that his objective will be attained soon. If the animal is on his right then he still has a long way to go.

The Virtues of the Pig

Honest, making a virtue of simplicity, straightforward, pure spirited, diligent, calm, understanding, gallant

The Vices of the Pig

Gullible, easily swindled, willful, obstinate, prone to lust and depravity

The Pig Personality

The happy-go-lucky Pig will attract popularity by his open attitude and affectionate nature. He is equally sought after because when anyone is in need, it is invariable a person born under the sign of the kindly Pig who will offer assistance and emotional support. Pig personalities are often thought to be reserved when one first encounters them, and this is because they are emotionally vulnerable and they need time to gain confidence with strangers. However, as time progresses, a warm and cheerful character emerges. A Pig has few close friends with whom he shares his thoughts, even though his circle of acquaintances will be wide.

There is an innocence and naivety in the Pig personality, which though attractive, can also put in danger of being conned, swindled and otherwise deceived. This trait, combined with eagerness for novelty, makes Pig personalities yearn for new experiences and it encourages them to travel widely.

It is this eagerness that can make Pigs tactless or encourage them to behave in an inappropriate manner. Even so, it is easy to forgive the Pig simply because he has no malice in him.

The Pig in Love

It is in the area of romance that Pig personalities are at their most vulnerable. It is necessary for them to experiment, to be outgoing and meet potential mates, but there is the ever present danger that these people are unsuitable and self seeking, or willing to take advantage of the Pig's good nature. It is a good thing that Pigs are quick learners and rarely make the same mistake twice. At least when a suitable partner is found the Pig will be absolutely sure that this is indeed the right one!

Pigs are very tolerant and they will be quietly amused by the personal foibles of their partners, but never make the mistake of thinking that the Pig has not noticed what is going on. He may seem to be dreaming his life away but he is actually very observant indeed. The Pig needs someone who will share his sense of fun, as well as recognizing his more serious and sensitive side.

The Pig is likely to find love with the refined Hare and the artistically gifted Goat.

The Pig's natural charm will win approval from most signs, particularly the Rat, Ox, Tiger, Dragon, Horse, Rooster, and Dog.

It is not considered wise for Pigs to consort with other Pigs because a sense of paranoia will emerge. The Snake will take advantage of the Pig's good nature while the Monkey and Pig have very little in common at all.

The Pig Career

Pigs are not traditionally thought to be ambitious and they are happiest when there exists a good equilibrium between home and work. Pigs are capable of competent work, but they prefer to find a comfortable rut and stay in it, rather than scaling the stressful ladder of success. A Pig finds it preferable to work in cooperation with others as part of an efficient team. The Pig is methodical and likes to know exactly where he is. Risks make Pigs extremely nervous so there is a tendency to err on the side of caution.

Pigs are suited to a career in medicine, teaching or the caring professions. The law or music may appeal to some, while others will prefer a more scientific role. Pigs find satisfaction as a writer, landscape gardener, artist, librarian, computer programmer or researcher.

The Pig and the Five Elements

The five ancient elements of Chinese tradition will provide an extra dimension to the tolerant Pig character.

The Wood Pig (1935, 1995)

The Wood Pig personality is a conventional one. The usual Pig characteristics of tolerance, intelligence and modesty are in evidence. This is a compassionate Pig who is always ready to help others who are less fortunate. This may be accomplished by cleverly manipulating people around to their way of thinking. However, the tendency to be gullible is also present. Wood Pigs often excel at athletics or writing.

The Fire Pig (1947, 2007)

The Fire Pig personality can be described as possessing an artistic temperament. This person tends to be highly-strung, a little eccentric, intensely emotional and possessed of high intuition and he can sometimes be quite psychic. The caring or medical professions attract Fire Pigs but some are more drawn to alternative therapies. This type of Pig is very popular, cheerful and fun loving, and devoted to his family. Fire Pigs tend to worry about relationships and finances. Under stress Fire Pigs can be obstinate, willful and something of a bully.

The Earth Pig (1959, 2019)

This is a sensible Pig who prides himself on his sound common sense and steady, productive habits. The Earth Pig type is not usually very ambitious, so he may rely on a tougher and more pragmatic partner. The Earth Pig type wants a quiet, ordinary, uncomplicated life. This Pig is devoted to his family and indeed to family values. He is careful with money, but that does not stop him being extremely fond of food and drink.

The Metal Pig (1971)

The Metal Pig is the most ambitious individual born under this sign. Indeed, he can be forceful, domineering and determined to get his own way. He is more extrovert than the usual Pig and he can be extremely sociable but he always keeps something back from his acquaintances. He can be moody and he certainly needs periods of solitude. Emotionally, this Pig is possessive very protective of friends and family.

The Water Pig (1983)

The Water Pig possesses a dreamy nature and he is creative and artistic. The Watery type of Pig doesn't mind some financial insecurity as long as he can express his creativity and be allowed the peace to dream. As might be imagined, he is very sensitive indeed; also romantic, very caring and so emotional that he is easily upset. Water Pigs love travel and can regale an audience with tall tales of their adventures. This Pig is not ambitious but he is very sensuous and prone to over-indulge himself.

The Year of the Pig

This is the last of the Animal Signs, so it can be taken as a celestial message to tie up loose ends, come to terms with all that has happened in the last twelve years and to prepare for a new beginning. It may be a period marked by nostalgia and a few regrets. Having said that, it is important that positive influences and events should be paramount. In other words, the Pig Year is one in which every one of us can assess how far we've come, count our blessings and consider our next moves. Of course those who have squandered their opportunities throughout the Animal Sign cycle may think very differently now.

In essence, there is feeling of celebration, and in common with the symbolism of the fun loving Pig, this could be a time for self-indulgence and enjoying the finer things of life. The kindly Pig also looks with favor on romance, so amorous adventures will be fortunate. Family and domestic issues will prove to be favorable.

Even though anything as strenuous as political upheaval is unlikely, there may still be a revolution in ideas and concepts in the Pig Year. However, this change is most likely to occur in leisure activities and it may bring a change in the way that vast numbers of people spend their recreation time.

The Fortunes of the Pig Year by Year

The Pig in the Rat Year: There should be optimism in the air while the Pig takes a successful path in the Year of his friend, the Rat. However, it is important for the Pig to resist complacency, because the rat favors the enterprising and the bold. The Pig should pick a goal and slowly aim at it. Results may not be immediate but the eventual rewards will be very great indeed.

The Pig in the Ox Year: The Year of the Ox calls for hard work, and fortunately the Pig is up to the task. Even though there will be some hardship along the way, the outlook is still good. As long as the pleasure-loving side of the Pig's personality doesn't gain dominance, there is a lot to be gained this year. So all a wise Pig has to watch out for is a tendency to alienate his colleagues by overindulging himself.

The Pig in the Tiger Year: The turbulent Year of the Tiger is not a comfortable one for the often-timid Pig. All the revolutionary changes are very unsettling even when the Pig actually sympathizes with the aims. To avoid anxiety the Pig should stand back, follow his own concerns and try to let the world's events pass him by. This attitude will ensure popularity, for the Pig will be much sought after and his laid-back personality will provide respite for others in this fraught time.

The Pig in the Hare Year: The outlook for the Pig's cash reserves look pretty good in the compatible Year of the Hare. If you'll excuse the pun, it's a "piggy-bank" year. Of course, with all this extra affluence, the self-indulgent Pig can afford a more opulent lifestyle, and he will be determined to get one! He must take care not to be over generous though. The Pig's personality gains some strength so he will be able to stand up for himself and cut a more forceful figure during this twelve-month period.

The Pig in the Dragon Year: Financial good fortune continues in the ostentatious Dragon Year. However, the Pig may find himself ill at ease and may even feel a little guilty that everything seems to be going his way while other people suffer. Many Pigs have a sneaking suspicion that something underhanded and sneaky is going on, and even worse, that they are an unwitting part of it. Pigs will also feel that times are about to change and there may be some payback up ahead.

The Pig in the Snake Year: Let caution be a Pig's watchword in the year of his enemy, the Snake. Nothing is straightforward or as it seems to be. No business deal will be completely above-board and no potential relationship will be emotionally sound. This is going to be an anxious time for the vulnerable Pig, and this is made even worse by the fact that nothing will be satisfactorily explained.

The Pig in the Horse Year: The Pig's fraught nerves can relax a little in the Year of the Horse. Having been through any number of emotional traumas, this is a chance for him to recuperate. During this period, there will be a lot of analysis and self-doubt, but even so, the Pig's fortunes are rising. Those Pigs who have been thwarted in love will find that situation changing rapidly for the better.

The Pig in the Goat Year: The pressure seems to be off when the Year of the Goat comes around. This is not the most exciting of years, but then again, that's exactly the way a Pig will like it. Finances will be steady and heady romance will give way to simple contentment.

The Pig in the Monkey Year: The Monkey and the Pig are incompatible signs so this is not going to be one of the Pig's better years. There are intrigues going on, and the Pig will be hard-pressed to keep up with all the twists and turns around him. It may also be too risky for comfort, so a wise Pig will take care, make preparations and hold to his own decisions and principles.

The Pig in the Rooster Year: The Year of the strutting Rooster will bring a much-needed lesson in economy and financial planning. It will go to show that, although the best things in life are not necessarily free, they are certainly cheaper. In this period, the

Pig enters a more controlled phase and he can develop his more cultural, refined tastes.

The Pig in the Dog Year: The year of the idealistic Dog may initially sound promising but it's too full of well-meaning crusaders to give the Pig much peace. Pigs should not be taken in by promises and they should demand proof of all claims. The lives of those around the Pig will be full of turmoil, so he will have to learn to say no and to separate himself from disruptive influences if he is to have any peace at all.

The Pig in the Pig Year: An increase in personal confidence will come as a blessed relief to Pigs in their own year. Fortune smiles on the Pig now and many opportunities will come his way. Many Pigs will embark on a long-term relationship with a person who not only understands them but also allows them some breathing space. For many, this emotional link will be a secret affair. Other Pigs will move to a new home or start a family. Good fortune decrees financial successes in business or at work.